W9-COG-729

ALCHEMY

ALCHEMY
The Secret Art

STANISLAS KLOSSOWSKI DE ROLA

THAMES AND HUDSON

ART AND IMAGINATION
General Editor: Jill Purce

Any copy of this book issued by the publisher as a paperback
is sold subject to the condition that it shall not by way of
trade or otherwise be lent, resold, hired out or otherwise
circulated without the publisher's prior consent in any
form of binding or cover other than that in which it is
published and without a similar condition including these
words being imposed on a subsequent purchaser:

© 1973 Thames and Hudson Ltd, London

Published in the United States in 1985 by
Thames and Hudson Inc., 500 Fifth Avenue,
New York, New York 10110

Library of Congress Catalog Card Number 85–50803

All Rights Reserved. No part of this publication may be
reproduced or transmitted in any form or by any means,
electronic or mechanical, including photocopy, recording or
any other information storage and retrieval system, without
prior permission in writing from the publisher.

Printed and bound in Yugoslavia

Contents

Introduction

THIS book is an attempt to show, within a limited space, a glimpse of what true alchemy was and is. Most modern dictionaries have lent currency to popular misconceptions by dismissing it as an immature, empirical and speculative precursor of chemistry which had as its object the transmutation of base metals into gold. But, although chemistry did evolve from alchemy, the two sciences have extremely little in common. Whereas chemistry deals with scientifically verifiable phenomena, the mysterious doctrine of alchemy pertains to a hidden reality of the highest order which constitutes the underlying essence of all truths and all religions. The perfection of this essence is termed the Absolute; it can be perceived and realized, as the Beauty of all Beauty, the Love of all Love and the High Most High, only if consciousness is radically altered and transmuted from the ordinary (lead-like) level of everyday perception to a subtle (gold-like) level of perception, so that every object is perceived in its perfect archetypal form, which is contained within the Absolute. The realization of the eternal perfection of everything everywhere constitutes the Universal Redemption. Alchemy is a rainbow bridging the chasm between the earthly and heavenly planes, between matter and spirit. Like the rainbow, it may appear within reach, only to recede if one chases it merely to find a pot of gold.

   The sacred, secret, ancient and profound science of alchemy, the royal or sacerdotal art, also called the hermetic philosophy, conceals, in esoteric texts and enigmatic emblems, the means of penetrating the very secrets of Nature, Life and Death, of Unity, Eternity and Infinity.

Viewed in the context of these secrets, that of gold-making is, relatively speaking, of little consequence: something comparable to the super-powers (siddhis) sometimes obtained by Great Yogis, which are not sought after for their own sake, but are important by-products of high spiritual attainment.

To begin with, therefore, we shall consider what it was that alchemists actually sought to achieve. 'Alchemy is not merely an art or science to teach metallic transmutation, so much as a true and solid science that teaches how to know the centre of all things, which in the divine language is called the Spirit of Life.' (Pierre-Jean Fabre, *Les Secrets chymiques*, Paris 1636.)

However, the transmutative process, without being the final end, is an indispensable part of the Great Work – the *Magnum Opus* – which is, at one and the same time, a material and a spiritual realization. This fact is very often overlooked in alchemical studies. Some commentators claim alchemy to be wholly a spiritual discipline, while others seem interested only in finding out whether gold was actually made and by whom.

Both attitudes are misleading. It is essential to keep in mind that there are precise correspondences, fundamental to alchemical thought, between the visible and the invisible, above and below, matter and spirit, planets and metals. Gold, because of its incorruptible nature and its remarkable physical characteristics, is to alchemists the Sun of matter, an analogy to the ultimate perfection which they themselves seek to attain by helping 'base' metals to reach the blessed state of gold. As gold is also, in a sense, the shadow of the Sun, the Sun is the shadow of God.

'The Great Work is, above all things, the creation of man by himself, that is to say, the full and entire conquest of his faculties and his future; it is especially the perfect emancipation of his will, assuring him universal dominion over Azoth and the domain of Magnesia, in other words, full power over the Universal Magical Agent. This Agent, disguised by the ancient philosophers under the name of the First Matter, determines the forms of modifiable substance, and we can really arrive by means of it at metallic transmutation and the Universal Medicine.' (Eliphas Levi, *Transcendental Magic*, London.)

Throughout history, true alchemists, disdainful of wealth and worldly honours, have actively sought the Universal Medicine, the Panacea, which, ultimately sublimated, becomes the Fountain of Youth, the Elixir of Life and the Key to Immortality in both a spiritual and a mysterious physical sense. The Elixir would not only cure all ills by uprooting the causes of disease, but it would also rejuvenate and finally transmute the human body into an incorruptible 'body of light'.

The Adept (*adeptus*, 'he who has attained' the Gift of God) would then be crowned with the triple crown of Enlightenment: Omniscience, Omnipotence, and the Joy of Divine Eternal Love. But many are called and few chosen; it is only fair to say that very few among the few have succeeded in reaching the ultimate goal. These are the Brotherhood of Light, and are Alive.

Before obtaining the Elixir, the alchemist has first to triumph over all the obstacles and difficulties of an extremely intricate process which culminates in the production of the Philosophers' Stone. It is this so-called Stone that has the property of transmuting base metals into gold. Consequently, most alchemical texts seem to deal exclusively with the preparation of the Stone and of minor medicines.

Though full of promises, these texts invariably contain elaborate devices to deter the unworthy. They are couched in a language often so obscure and so impenetrable that their study requires years and years of devoted attention, of reading and re-reading, before their exegesis may even be attempted. For secrecy is inextricably woven into the fabric of alchemy, and is still invoked by modern alchemists.

Sceptics and believers will be found to agree that, had the alchemists spoken clearly, they would, throughout history, have been persecuted for their unconventional ideas and beliefs. But where the two sides begin to differ is that while the former deny the existence of any practical basis to alchemy and therefore dismiss its secrecy as a veil to hide ignorance, the latter claim that, in part at least, secrecy was necessary in order to ensure that the knowledge of devastating forces should not fall into the wrong hands.

There are, however, other reasons for the obscurity of the alchemical texts: they constitute a challenge to the heroic nature of him who seeks to 'innerstand'. Like Theseus, the enquirer confronts the Labyrinth. This Labyrinth is a defiance of linear logic, which in this context is totally useless. The assault on the logical sense is made by the Minotaur of the absurd, who will promptly rout the would-be hero who cannot withstand his attack. Only through reliance on inspired intuition, the golden thread of Ariadne, will the puzzle fall into place and light replace darkness. Such methods, by which the limitations of the mind are bypassed or transcended, are used by the esoteric masters of many a spiritual discipline. Zen masters, for instance, use the koans, a kind of riddle, which, while unbalancing the intellect, may suddenly trigger satori or enlightenment.

But despite the tremendous difficulties which Eastern and Western esoteric doctrines present, those that arise before the student of alchemy surpass them all. Especially if he wishes to go beyond the surface periodically skimmed by historians, psychologists and other scholars.

If the approach to alchemy through its texts is indeed forbidding, the despondent seeker can find in alchemical art a way, fraught with wonder, into the heart of the subject. For in their images alchemists have spoken in ingenious and often very beautiful ways of things about which they have never written.

This pictorial language, in which not a single detail is ever meaningless, exerts a deep fascination on the sensitive beholder. This fascination does not even necessarily depend upon understanding. If the reader will *contemplate* these images, that is to say go beyond their surface, he will often perceive that they correspond to another timeless dimension which we all may find deep within ourselves.

These profoundly haunting pictures have a polyvalent symbolism, and lend themselves therefore to various interpretations. As a result, deplorable controversies periodically arise between the exponents of different interpretations, with each claiming his own to be the only valid one. (To give only one example, the vehement denunciation of C. G. Jung's interpretations of alchemical symbolism in the recently published book of a noted alchemist is a show of narrow-minded and dogmatic intolerance of the worst kind.)

Alchemy cannot be bound to a single system of thought, any more than it can be reduced to a single symbolical interpretation, because it transcends all dogma and all religions. One must not forget that at one time or another, sometimes in turn and sometimes simultaneously, Chinese, Indians, Egyptians, Greeks and Arabs have practised the art. All of them contributed to making it what it ultimately became in medieval times; since then the so-called evolution of alchemical thought has been superficial and largely illusory.

The Great Work

The quest for the *Materia Prima* must be the disciple's first labour. 'Its traditional name, Stone of the Philosophers, sufficiently depicts this substance to serve as the basis of its identification. It is indeed veritably a stone, because it presents, when out of the mine, the same outward characteristics that are common to all ores.' (Fulcanelli, *Les Demeures Philosophales*.) This Stone of the Philosophers, the 'subject' of the art, is not to be confused with the Philosophers' Stone. The subject only becomes the Philosophers' Stone when, transformed and perfected by the art, it reaches its ultimate perfection and consequent transmutative quality.

In the alchemical literature, the *Materia Prima* is said to have an imperfect body, a constant soul, a penetrating tincture and a clear transparent mercury, volatile and mobile. It bears within its breast the gold of philosophers and the mercury of the wise. It is called by a multitude of names, but no alchemist has ever publicly revealed its true nature. One of the capital difficulties in alchemy is the identification of this matter. In alchemical texts, everything pertaining to the beginning of the Work is almost always omitted, or else described in a totally misleading way.

The whole of the Work is prepared and achieved with this single substance, which, once identified, must be secured. In order to do so, it is essential to journey to the mine, and to take possession of the raw subject. This is no small undertaking in itself, and the casting of a horoscope is necessary to determine the most favourable time. The Work may only be begun in the spring, under the signs of Aries, Taurus and Gemini (the most favourable time to begin being in Aries, the celestial hieroglyph of which corresponds, in the esoteric or steganographic language, to the name of the *Materia Prima*).

As a preliminary to the Work itself, the subject must be purified, rid of its attle. This is done by a means well known to metallurgists, which does, however, we are told, require great ingenuity, patience and labour.

Another operation is the preparation of the secret fire, *Ignis Innaturalis*, also called the natural fire. This secret fire, or First Agent, is described by alchemists as a dry water that does not wet the hands, and as a fire burning without flames. It has baffled and misled many; Pontanus admits to having erred more than two hundred times because of it. In fact, this substance is a salt, prepared from cream of tartar by a process which requires skill and a perfect knowledge of chemistry. The process involves the use of spring dew, collected by ingenious and poetical means and distilled.

The First Matter and First Agent of the Work having been prepared, the preliminaries are virtually over. The *Materia Prima* is placed in a mortar made of agate (or any other very hard substance), pulverized with a pestle, mixed with the secret fire, and moistened with dew.

The resulting 'compost' is then enclosed in a hermetically sealed vessel or Philosophic Egg, which is placed in the Athanor, the furnace of the Philosophers.

This Athanor is devised in such a way as to be able to keep the Egg at a constant temperature for long periods of time. The outward fire stimulates the action of the inner fire, and must therefore be restrained; otherwise, even if the vessel does not break, the whole work will be lost. In the initial stage the heat is compared to that of a hen sitting on her eggs. (In more ways than one, the natural process through which chickens are born is comparable to the alchemical process.)

In the Egg the two principles within the *Materia Prima* – one solar, hot and male, known as sulphur, the other lunar, cold and female, known as mercury – interact.

'These two then (which Avicen calleth the Corascene bitch and the Armenian dogge)', writes Nicolas Flamel, 'these two I say, being put together in the vessel of the sepulcher, doe bite one another cruelly, and by their great poyson, and furious rage, they never leave one another, from the moment that they have seized on one another (if the cold hinder them not) till both of them by their slavering venom, and mortall hurts, be all of a goarebloud, over all the parts of their bodies; and finally killing one another, be stewed in their proper venome, which after their death, changeth them into living and permanent water; before which time, they loose in their corruption and putrification, their first natural formes, to take afterwards one onely new, more noble, and better forme.'

Thus death, which is a separation, is followed by a long process of decay which lasts until all is putrefied and the opposites dissolved in the liquid *nigredo*. This darkness darker than darkness, this 'black of blacks', is the first sure sign that one is on the right path; hence the alchemical aphorism: 'No generation without corruption.'

The *nigredo* phase ends with the appearance on the surface of a starry aspect, which is likened to the night sky which told shepherds and kings that a child was born in Bethlehem. And so the first work, the first degree of perfection, nears completion when, from the mutual destruction of conjoint opposites, there appears the metallic, volatile humidity which is the Mercury of the Wise.

The volatile principle of mercury flies through the alchemical air, within the microcosm of the Philosophical Egg, 'in the belly of the wind', receiving the celestial and purifying influences above. It falls again, sublimated, on the New Earth which must eventually emerge. As the outer fire is very slowly intensified, the moist yields to the dry until the coagulation and desiccation of the emerging continent is complete. While this is happening, a great number of beautiful colours appear, corresponding to a stage known as the Peacock's Tail.

The end of the 'second work' comes with the appearance of the Whiteness, *albedo*. Once the Whiteness is reached, our subject is said to have acquired sufficient strength to resist the ardours of the fire, and it is only one step more until the Red King or Sulphur of the Wise appears out of the womb of his mother and sister, Isis or mercury, *Rosa Alba*, the White Rose.

The third work recapitulates the operations of the first, with a new significance. It begins with the pomp of a royal wedding. The King is reunited in the Fire of Love (the salt or secret fire) with his blessed Queen. Just as Cadmus pierced the serpent with his spear, the red sulphur fixes the white mercury; and from their reunion the ultimate perfection is effected, and the Philosophers' Stone is born.

To recapitulate, briefly:

There are three stones, or three works, or three degrees of perfection, within the Work.

The first work ends when the subject has been perfectly purified (by means of repeated distillation and solidification) and reduced into a pure mercurial substance.

The second degree of perfection is attained when our same subject has been cooked, digested and fixed into an incombustible sulphur.

The third stone appears when the subject has been fermented, multiplied and brought to the Ultimate Perfection, a fixed, permanent, tingent tincture: the Philosophers' Stone.

True and false alchemy

As the true aims of alchemy have always been disguised by the hermetic symbolism in which the lore of metallic transmutation is expressed, confusion and error inevitably ensue when uninitiated people attempt to interpret esoteric recipes too literally. Fascinated by the fatal mirage of gold, a motley breed of people whom true alchemists disdainfully call 'puffers' (because of their frantic use of the bellows), in ignorance of the true principles of the art, have performed a multitude of invariably unsuccessful and often disastrous experiments which have caused alchemy to be decried as the 'false art' and led Chaucer, among others, to scoff:

> *This cursed craft whoso wil exercise,*
> *He shal no gold have that may him suffise,*
> *For al the gold he spendeth thereaboute*
> *He lose shal, thereof I have no doute.*

The classic retort to this is given by Artephius: 'Poor fool! Will you be simple enough to believe that we teach openly and clearly the greatest and the most important of all secrets? I assure you that he who would explain, with the ordinary and literal meaning of words, what philosophers have written, shall find himself caught within the meanders of a labyrinth whence he shall never escape, because he will not have

Ariadne's thread to guide him out. And whatever he may spend, that much will be lost in working thus.'

Such warnings are frequent in alchemical texts, but the puffers paid them no heed; and in their folly quite often blew themselves up or were poisoned by noxious fumes. But one must credit to their foolhardiness some important chemical discoveries; and it has often been said that they, much more than the true alchemists, laid the foundations of organic chemistry.

Dom Pernety in his *Dictionnaire Mytho-Hermétique* declares: 'Most authors vary in their definition of this science, because there are two sorts [of alchemy], one true and the other false. . . . True alchemy consists in perfecting metals, and in the maintenance of health. False alchemy in destroying both the one and the other.

'The first employs Nature's agents and imitates her operations. The second works on erroneous principles and employs the tyrant and destroyer of Nature as her agent. The first, from a small quantity of a vile matter, fashions a most precious thing. The second, from a most precious matter, from gold itself, fashions a matter most vile, smoke and ashes. The result of the true [alchemy] is the prompt cure of all ills afflicting humanity; the result of the false consists in those same ills that commonly befall puffers.

'Alchemy has fallen into disrepute since a great number of bad artists have, with their swindles, deceived the gullible and the ignorant.

'Gold is the object of men's ambitions; the dangers to which one must expose oneself over land or sea, to procure this precious metal, rebuff but few.

'A man calls on one: he knows, he claims the means to accrue within one's own home the mother lode of all treasures, without any other risks than that of a part of those one possesses. On the strength of his words, the falsity of which remains unknown because one is in ignorance of the ways of Nature, one succumbs, one sows one's gold to reap but smoke; one ruins oneself, one ends up by hating the impostor and doubting the existence of alchemy, all because one failed to attain the intended goal by taking the road going the opposite way. . . .

'There are few artists who are true alchemists: there are many who work according to the principles of vulgar chemistry. The latter draw all manner of sophistry from this art, which provides for all those impostors, who, after having ruined themselves, seek to ruin others. [Their art] should be despised for all these reasons, if one did not have stronger reasons to value it, in view of the great number of its discoveries useful to society.

'True alchemists do not glory in their science; they do not seek to swindle or cheat other people out of their money, because, as Morien said to King Calid, he that has everything, needs nothing. They give of their goods to those in need. They sell not their secret: and if they transmit their knowledge to a few friends, it is only to those they deem worthy of possessing it and making use of it according to God's Will. They know Nature and its operations, and make use of this knowledge to reach, as St Paul says, that of the Creator.'

To reach the knowledge of the Creator is to part the veil and transmute the obscurity of ignorance into the light of wisdom. To attain that supreme wisdom is consciously to become one with God in love: to live to love. But how can man escape from the prison of his own imperfection? How can he transcend his present conditioning, to become God?

This is the question that ultimately confronts us when we consider the riddle of alchemy. He who would find the answer, not only intellectually but as a way of Life – indeed as a way *to* Life – must begin by taking a long, hard, unblinking look at himself. He will, if he is honest, see that the root cause of all of his troubles lies in his almost total ignorance of that which matters most: his true self.

Because of the total confusion between Ego and Self that clouds his spirit and dissipates his energy, man stumbles through life, spiritually blind to causes, struggling with effects. As a consequence he is not unlike the Mad King of whom it is told that he had retreated to the darkest *oubliette* in his palace and despite all entreaties refused to come out. Whenever his desperate ministers came down to try to persuade him to return and reign above, he would snarl at them. They would try to remind him of the beauty of his palace, of the wonders of his gardens, of his harem, of his friends all sorrowing at his absence. But no argument could penetrate his madness, and he would call them liars and accuse them of wanting to rob him of a worthless bundle of filthy rags which he called his possessions.

If what we own, instead of freedom, brings us bondage, what good is it to us? He who would be free must ask himself: 'What am I living for?' He must shake off the fateful conditioning that heredity, environment and society have given him, 'for within is the kingdom'.

'Any descent within oneself – any look within – is at the same time an Ascent – an Assumption – a look towards the true reality without. The renunciation of oneself is the source of all humility, as well as the basis of any true ascent. The first step is a look within, an exclusive contemplation of our very self. But he who stops there remains halfway. The second step must be an efficacious look without, an active, autonomous and persevering observation of the outside world. . . .

'We shall understand the world when we understand ourselves; for it and we are inseparable halves of one whole. We are children of God, divine seeds. One day, we shall be what our Father is.' (Novalis.)

Innerstanding

Everything comes from the One and returns to the One, by the One, for the One. Thus speaks, reassuringly, Ouroboros (a snake or dragon eating its own tail), the eloquent symbol of the Infinite Eternal One, which represents perfectly the Great Cycle of the universe, as well as the Great Work which reflects it: perfect stillness and perfect motion.

The solar hieroglyph of gold ($\odot$) expresses the same notion, and the legendary father of alchemy, Hermes Trismegistus, in his Emerald Table, calls alchemy the operation of the Sun:

'It is true without lie, certain and most veritable, that what is below is like what is above and that what is above is like what is below, to perpetrate the miracles of one thing.

'And as all things have been, and come from One by the meditation of One; thus all things have been born from this single thing by adaptation.

'The Sun is its father and the Moon its mother.

'The Wind has carried it in his belly and the Earth is its nurse. The father of all the perfection [*Telesmus*] of all the world is here.

'Its force or power is entire if it is turned into earth.

'Thou shalt separate the Earth from the Fire, the subtle from the gross, softly, with great ingenuity.

'It rises from the Earth to the sky and again descends into the Earth, and receives the force of things superior and inferior.

'Thou shalt have by this means the glory of all the world. And therefore all obscurity shall flee from thee.

'And this is the strength strong of all strength. For it shall vanquish any thing subtle and anything solid penetrate.

'Thus the world is created.

'From this shall be and shall proceed admirable adaptations, of which the means is here.

'And in this connection I am called Hermes Trismegistus, having the three parts of the philosophy of all the world.

'It is finished, what I have said of the operation of the Sun.'

This Emerald Table has always been highly considered by alchemists of all centuries. They make constant references to it, and from it are derived a great number of frequently quoted aphorisms, such as 'As Above So Below'. It confirms the analogies between the macrocosm represented by the circle ○ and the microcosm represented by the axial point · (Sanskrit bindu), without which the Infinite would remain uncreated, incomplete, centreless. In seeking to interpret the Emerald Table it is important not to jump to hasty conclusions, and above all not to limit its meaning to one level of understanding. The further one grows in the knowledge of the principles of this art, the richer one becomes in *intuitive* comprehension, or 'innerstanding'. This naturally applies to all alchemical texts, but more so here than anywhere else. The student will at first be intrigued, then will be tempted to dismiss the whole thing as gibberish (the latter word, ironically enough, derives from the dismissal of Jabir or Geber the Arab alchemist's work as unintelligible); then, if he is patient and humble enough (alchemists say that patience is the ladder of philosophers, and humility the key to their garden), the first intuitive sparks igniting in his spirit will encourage him to continue until he begins to be able to separate the subtle from the gross, the true from the false. One must proceed with care, 'softly, with great ingenuity'.

This process of patient elucidation is illustrated by the commentary on the Emerald Table written by a fourteenth-century Adept, Hortulanus, the Gardener (*ab ortis maritimis nuncupatus*, 'so-called from the maritime gardens'):

'I. The philosopher says: *It is true*, that is that the art of alchemy was given to us. *Without lie*, he says this to confound those who say that the science is a lie or false. *Certain*, that is to say experienced, for any thing experienced is most certain. *And most veritable*. For the most veritable Sun is procreated by the art. He says *most veritable*, in a superlative degree, for the Sun begotten through this art exceeds all natural Sun in all medicinal and other properties. [Hortulanus here means that the alchemical gold of philosophers far excels common, natural or vulgar gold.]

'II. Consequently he touches upon the operation of the Stone, saying *that what is below is like what is above*. He says this because the Stone is divided into two principal parts by the *Magisterium* [the Work], into the superior part that rises above, and the inferior part that remains below, fixed and clear. [Here reference is made to the separation from the original chaos of two principles, the volatile or essence, which rises in the vessel, and the fixed or dense matter. The former is often called the spirit and the latter body.]

'And however these two parts are concordant in virtue. And for this he says *that what is above is like what is below*.

'This division is certainly necessary. *To perpetrate the miracles of one thing*, that is to say the Stone. For the inferior part is the Earth which is called the nurse and ferment; and the superior part is the soul, which vivifies and resuscitates the whole Stone. And for this the separation is made, the conjunction celebrated, and many miracles come to be perpetrated and done within the secret work of Nature.

'III. *And as all things have been, and come from One by the meditation of One*. He gives here an example saying: *As all have been, and come from One*, that is to say, from a chaotic globe, or a chaotic mass. *By the meditation*, that is to say by the cogitation and creation of One, that is to say Almighty God. *Thus all things have been born*. That is to say have sprung. *From this single thing*, that is to say from a confused mass [the *Materia Prima*].

'*By adaptation*, that is to say by the sole commandment and miracle of God. Thus our Stone is born and sprung from a confused mass, containing within itself all the elements, which has been created by God, and by his sole miracle is our Stone sprung and born.'

In the evocative words of the Emerald Table, and of its commentary (of which only a small part can be quoted here), we have a diagram or symbolic map of the alchemical operation. Naturally the traveller must learn to interpret the map, otherwise he will get hopelessly lost. First we must assume that we have obtained the hidden, unrevealed, chaotic *Materia Prima*, 'our chaos'. This is always likened to the state of the world at the beginning of Genesis, before the constitution and separation of all things into distinct elements. It will thus be clear that the alchemical process is a microcosmic reconstitution of the process of creation, in other words a re-creation. It is effected by the interplay of forces symbolized by two dragons, one black and one white, locked in an eternal circular combat. The white one is winged, or volatile, the black one wingless, or fixed; they are accompanied by the universal alchemical formula *solve et coagula*. This formula and this emblem symbolize the alternating role of the two indispensable halves that compose the Whole. *Solve et coagula* is an injunction to alternate *dissolution*, which is a spiritualization or sublimation of solids, with *coagulation*, that is to say a re-materialization of the purified products of the first operation. Its cyclic aspect is clearly expressed by Nicolas Valois: '*Solvite corpora et coagulate spiritum*': 'Dissolve the body and coagulate the spirit.'

In the words of Hermes Trismegistus: 'Thou shalt separate the Earth from the Fire' (this refers to the separation of the solid and subtle states of sulphur), 'the subtle from the gross, softly, with great ingenuity'. 'It rises from the Earth to the sky [*solve*] and again descends into the Earth [*coagula*] and receives the force of things superior and inferior.'

The Earth is in a broad sense our Matter, or *Mater*, the Mother from whom all corporeal things take their source. '*Terra enim est mater Elementorum; de terra procedunt et ad terram revertuntur,*' says Hermes: 'The Earth is the Mother of the Elements; from the Earth they proceed, to the Earth they return.' 'Make the Earth light, and give weight to the Fire, if you would meet what is rarely met,' says another; while in *La Fontaine des amoureux* we find:

> *Si fixum solvas faciasque volatile fixum,*
> *Et volucrem figas, faciet te vivere tutum:*

'If you dissolve the fixed, and make fixed the volatile, and make fast the winged thing, it will make you live safely.' From the interplay of the Four Elements, and their metamorphosis one into the other, all is evolved, and the fifth element, the Quintessence, distilled.

The Four and the Three

The monk Ferrarius defines alchemy as 'the science of the Four Elements, which are to be found in all created substances but are not of the vulgar kind. The whole practice of the art is simply the conversion of these Elements into one another.'

'Know then', says Nicolas Flamel in his *Thresor de Philosophie*, 'that this science is knowledge of the Four Elements, and of their seasons and qualities, mutually and reciprocally changed one into the other: on that the philosophers are all in agreement.

'And know that beneath the sky, there are Four Elements, not visible to sight, but by effect, by the means of which the philosophers under the cover of the elementary doctrine, have given and shown this science.'

Aristotle, often quoted in alchemical texts, pointed out that the link between the Four Elements was through their properties, such as hot and cold, dry or humid:

> Heat + Dryness = Fire
> Heat + Humidity = Air
> Cold + Dryness = Earth
> Cold + Humidity = Water

Whether the Greek philosophers taught that the principle of all things was Water, like Thales, or Air, like Anaximander, or Air and Water, like Xenophanes, or the Four Elements, Earth, Water, Air, Fire, as did the school of Hippocrates, the tendency of Greek speculation was to establish the profound distinctions which resulted in the theory of the four elements, the four humours of the human body, etc, which the disciples of Aristotle held. Hippocrates contended that if man were composed of a single element, he would never be ill; but as he is composed of several elements, complex remedies are required. The theory of the four elements and the Oriental idea of the transmutation of elements were syncretized at Alexandria and finally developed by the Arab alchemists Jabir (Geber), Razi (Rhasis) and Ibn Sina (Avicenna).

The resulting amalgam has persisted to this day, weathering the scoffs of nineteenth-century atomism. Many of the basic ideas of alchemy developed among the Greek philosophers. Thus, Heraclitus of Ephesus, surnamed 'the Obscure', maintained that fire alone was the principle of all things; he regarded generation as an ascending road, i.e. a volatilization; and decomposition as a descending road, i.e. a fixation. Empedocles, who was the first to mention the Four Elements, subordinated them as complex products to his primordial indestructible atoms, animated by love and hatred. Democritus, investing these atoms with a movement of their own, proceeded to construct the universe by shocks and harmonies of shocks or vortices. And Anaxagoras saw 'the all in all' (Aristotle: *Meteorologica*, 4, 5), the infinitely great universe in the infinitely small atom, and ingeniously applied the principle of analogy to unravel the tangled skein of ancient science.

It was Aristotle himself who added to the four elements a fifth, Ether, eternal and unchangeable, itself the Prime Mover of the universe (*De Caelo*, 1, 2). In the fourth century AD, Nemesius, Bishop of Emesa, was one of the most distinguished representatives of Alexandrian syncretism. One quotation from his *Nature of Man* will suffice to show that the idea of the transmutation of metals, from the time when Platonism, Magic and Christianity were combined, was regarded as an article of orthodox belief: 'To prevent the destruction of elements, the Creator has wisely ordained that elements should be capable of transmutation one into the other, or into their component parts, or that their component parts should be resolved again into their original elements. Thus the perpetuity of things is secured by the continual succession of these reciprocal generations.'

The study of Gnosticism would carry us too far afield; but one more passage from this unjustly forgotten writer will serve to show how deeply all science was then imbued with mysticism. 'Porphyry, in his treatise on sensation, tells us that vision is produced neither by a cone nor an image, nor any other object, but that the mind, being placed in a rapport with visible objects, sees itself in these objects, which are nothing else than itself, seeing that the mind embraces everything, and that all that exists is nothing but the mind, which contains bodies of all kinds.'

This remarkable statement (which is echoed in Tibetan mysticism) is the cornerstone upon which rests the edifice of magical alchemy, the purpose of which is to attain to a realization of the perfect archetypes of the absolute.

In spite of all the evidence, there are still those who deny that connections exist between alchemy and esoteric Eastern doctrines. There has indeed been misuse of the word 'Tantra' in this connection; and it would be misleading to speak of alchemy simply as 'Western Tantrism'. But Indian alchemy (Rasayana) does exist; furthermore, a number of Tibetan Tantric concepts are closely related to esoteric Taoism, and Taoism in its turn is inseparable from Chinese alchemy. So, although one must proceed with caution, the open-minded will find a certain profit in the study of the analogies between alchemy and the Tantras (both Hindu and Buddhist).

Albert Poisson, in an interesting work entitled *Théorie et symboles des Alchimistes* (Paris 1891), concludes his study of the Four Elements with the following table, which shows the correspondences between the *Materia Prima*, the three principles of the art, and the Four Elements.

	SULPHUR	Earth (visible, solid state)
	Fixed principle	Fire (occult, subtle state)
MATERIA PRIMA SINGLE AND INDESTRUCTIBLE	SALT	Quintessence, state comparable to the ether of the physicists
	MERCURY	Water (visible, liquid state)
	Volatile principle	Air (occult, gaseous state)

In alchemical terminology it can be said that, in a way, all liquids are water, all solids earth, and all vaporous or volatile substances air, while any kind of heat is fire. This is not, as some have supposed, an oversimplification due either to ignorance or to stupidity. Such a patronizing view evidences once more a purely literal interpretation of the terms employed, despite all the warning phrases such as Ferrarius' 'not of the vulgar kind'. It will one day be recognized that the old alchemists possessed a knowledge of the structure of matter and its properties far exceeding in refinement that of today's atom-smashers.

From the Four ($+$) we shall now consider the Three. As we have seen in Poisson's table, the Chaos or *Materia Prima* contains the three unrealized principles or potentialities of the Great Work: sulphur, salt and mercury. This Trinity of Matter corresponds to Spirit, Body and Soul, in the Microcosm of Man, and to Father, Son and Holy Ghost in the Macrocosm of God. Should the reader prefer to dispense with Christian terms, he may replace them by, for instance, the Unmanifested Principle, or Formless Void, called in Sanskrit Sunyata; the Manifested Creation, Reality or Sensible World, called in Sanskrit Maya; and that mysterious, subtle life energy called in Sanskrit Prana, which sustains all that lives.

In each of the three regions, the three principles (the Trinity) are three aspects of one thing: Unity.

This unity is unmanifested and therefore unknown, just as the fundamental unity of the three kingdoms (animal, vegetable and mineral) is unknown. The Great Work consists in a manifestation of this fundamental unity of the three kingdoms, in the three kingdoms. It consists in making known or visible what is occult, subtle and invisible, and in making occult, subtle and invisible what is known and visible.

Present and future

There seems to be an ever greater number of people interested in alchemy; and this is a good sign, a necessary shift from purely material goals toward a rediscovery of spiritual values. But no one should be deluded by this phenomenon; very few among the many will ever acquire a sufficiently sound theoretical foundation to become alchemists.

The problems connected with the undertaking of the Great Work are in themselves so great that they would in any case deter most of the unworthy. The first one is that most people probably still refuse to believe that anything is attainable by alchemical means. They object, for instance, to the necessity of performing certain operations at certain precise astrological periods, on the grounds that in chemistry no such things exist, and a proven experiment invariably yields the same results whether performed here or there, today or tomorrow. But in alchemy nothing is ever sure; one depends upon celestial influences, atmospheric conditions and all manner of waves and variations. Alchemy is not unlike agriculture, with which it is often compared; it is even called by some 'celestial agriculture'. This analogy comes from the fact that in agriculture one is dependent upon the seasons to plough, sow and reap. It would be absurd to expect results should one be demented enough to disregard the natural order of things. 'Just as God produces the grain in the fields, and it is then for us to make it into flour, to knead it and to make bread from it, our art requires that we do the same.'

The second problem is again a question of faith. What is at stake? Gold making? Who, today, would be gullible enough to believe that one might grow rich by alchemical means? Alchemy requires a considerable investment, if only to procure the necessary apparatus. Surely no puffer could now induce a businessman to invest a penny in such absurdities. Investment of capital requires the tangible prospect of a healthy return, and this is something no speculator would be crazy enough to fall for.

Besides, whether one believes in the reality of metallic transmutation or not, there are plenty of ways of obtaining gold which are safer and cheaper than alchemy. If gold and wealth are his goals, the seeker is well advised to look elsewhere.

Universal Medicine? Panacea? Elixir of Life? This proposition meets with an even more widespread scepticism. Yet Armand Barbault, a contemporary alchemist, achieved after twelve years what he calls in his book *L'Or du millième matin* (Paris 1969) the 'vegetable gold' or Elixir of the first degree.

This elixir was thoroughly analysed and tested by German and Swiss laboratories and doctors. It proved its great value and efficacy, especially in the treatment of very serious heart and kidney ailments. But it could not be fully analysed nor therefore synthesized. Its preparation required such peculiar care, and took so long, that eventually all hopes of commercialization were abandoned. The scientists who examined it declared that they were in the presence of a new state of matter having mysterious and perhaps deeply significant qualities. Meanwhile Barbault, helped by his wife and son, goes on working towards the second degree.

Eugène Canseliet, a distinguished writer and contemporary alchemist, the heir and disciple of Fulcanelli, has been diligently working towards the Great Work for over fifty years now. He has been able to attempt the last phase, called the third work, only four times in the last twenty years, and by his own admission he has failed. He attributes the limited number of attempts to unfavourable atmospheric conditions, and his failures (presumably) ultimately to himself. In his last book he concludes thus: 'One must wait and deserve the great miracle; to hold oneself ready, each spring, to utilize the unforeseeable week of weeks – *hebdomas hebdomadum* – when, exceptionally, the work of man and that of Nature shall meet.

'Let the student keep constantly in mind, as we do, that our quest is great beyond all other.

'In courage, humility and patience, it matters that the alchemist should not let himself be caught unawares.' (*L'Alchimie expliquée sur ses textes classiques*, Paris 1972.)

It is obvious that the number of people wise enough, or mad enough, to undertake such an unpromising task, and to accept all kinds of sacrifices, must indeed be very small. But it seems clear that if an 'unworthy' person were to persevere, and reach his goal despite all the difficulties, he would no longer be unworthy. Our own friend and teacher Lama Anagarika Govinda used to delight us with tales to that effect. Here is one:

A robber, having encountered one of the eighty-four Siddhas (Tantric masters who possess super-powers or siddhis), asked him by what means he might obtain a certain magic sword which would make him invincible and enable him to become the master of the whole world. The Siddha prescribed him a very arduous saddhana (spiritual and physical discipline) which he had to follow exactly in order to gain the magic sword. This saddhana the robber performed assiduously and fervently, so determined was he to gain the sword. After the prescribed number of years, he went to the appointed spot, a stupa, where he was told the sword would appear. He performed the ritual circumambulations, recited the mantras, and just as promised the sword appeared. As he grasped its handle he was enlightened, and at that very instant he had no more need of the magic sword.

In his *Foundations of Tibetan Mysticism* (London) Lama Govinda tells some of these stories and writes: 'The relationship between the highest and the ordinary state of consciousness was compared by certain schools of alchemy to that between the diamond and an ordinary piece of coal. One cannot imagine a greater contrast, and yet both consist of the same chemical substance, namely, carbon. This teaches symbolically the fundamental unity of all substances and their inherent faculty of transformation.

'To the alchemist who was convinced of the profound parallelism between the material and the immaterial world, and of the uniformity of natural and spiritual laws, this faculty of transformation had a universal meaning. It could be applied to inorganic forms of matter as well as to organic forms of life, and equally to the psychic forces that penetrate both. Thus, this miraculous power of transformation went far beyond what the crowd imagined to be the Philosophers' Stone, which was supposed to fulfil all wishes (even stupid ones!), or the Elixir of Life, which guaranteed an unlimited prolongation of earthly life. He who experiences this transformation has no more desires, and the prolongation of earthly life has no more importance for him who already lives in the deathless.

'This is emphasized over and over again in the stories of the Siddhas. Whatever is gained by way of miraculous powers loses in the moment of attainment all interest for the adept, because he has grown beyond the worldly aims which made the attainment of powers desirable. In this case, as in most others, it is not the end which sanctifies the means, but the means which sanctify the end by transforming it into a higher aim.'

An Exposition *upon Sir George Ripley's Vision*

written by Æyrenaeus Philalethes, Anglus, Cosmopolita

This text, first published in London in 1677, is a beautiful as well as instructive example of alchemical writing. Ripley, a fifteenth-century Adept, wrote his 'Vision' in a book, *The Twelve Gates*, on which the great and mysterious Æyrenaeus Philalethes commented in a series of treatises published under the title *Ripley Revived*. Philalethes is admired by all alchemists; his identity has been the subject of much speculation. His *Secret Entrance into the Shut Palace of the King* is a classic in English, Latin and French.

THE
VISION
OF
SIR GEORGE RIPLEY,
Canon of *Bridlington*, Unfolded.

When busie at my Book I was upon a certain Night,
This Vision *here exprest appear'd unto my dimmed sight:*
A Toad full Ruddy I saw, did drink the juice of Grapes so fast,
Till over-charged with the broth, his Bowels all to brast:
And after that, from poyson'd Bulk he cast his Venom fell,
For Grief and Pain whereof his Members all began to swell;
With drops of Poysoned sweat approaching thus his secret Den,
His Cave with blasts of fumous Air he all bewhited then:
And from the which in space a Golden Humour did ensue,
Whose falling drops from high did stain the soyl with ruddy hue.
And when his Corps the force of vital breath began to lack,
This dying Toad became forthwith like Coal for colour Black:
Thus drowned in his proper veins of poysoned flood;
For term of Eighty days and Four he rotting stood
By Tryal then this Venom to expel I did desire;
For which I did commit his Carkass to a gentle Fire:
Which done, a Wonder to the sight, but more to be rehearst;
The Toad with Colours rare through every side was pierc'd;
And White appear'd when all the sundry hews were past:
Which after being tincted Ruddy, for evermore did last.
Then of the Venom handled thus a Medicine I did make;
Which Venom kills, and saveth such as Venom chance to take:
Glory be to him the granter of such secret ways,
Dominion, and Honour both, with Worship, and with Praise. *Amen.*

This Vision is a Parable rather or Enigm, which the Ancient Wise Philosophers have been wont to use often in setting out their secrets; this Liberty is granted to all men for to make use of Enigmatical expressions, to decipher that which is indeed mysterious. The Ancient *Egyptians* taught much by Hieroglyphicks, which way many Fathers of this Science have followed; but most especially they have made use of Mystical or Cabalistical descriptions; such is this. But to the thing in hand.

A Toad full ruddy I saw. —

Here we have a Toad described, and in it the whole secret of Philosophers: The Toad is Gold; so called, because it is an Earthly Body, but most especially for the black stinking venenosity which this operation comes to in the first days of its preparation, before the whiteness appear; during the Rule of *Saturn*, therefore it is called the ruddy Toad.

To this Authors assent with one accord; when they say our stone is nothing else but Gold digested unto the highest degree, to which Nature and Art, can bring it; and again the first work, saith another Philosopher, is to sublime *Mercury*, and then into clean *Mercury* to put clean bodies: many witnesses I could bring, yea the whole current of writers run this way: And what if some subtle *Philosophers* seem to deny this, on purpose to deceive the unwary? We shall not make it our work to reconcile them; (though we might) for many of them wrote very enviously, on purpose to ensnare; all of them wrote mysteriously, as much as they could to darken the truth: and at the best none of them were but men, and described things according to their apprehensions in Philosophy, none of them wrote in every thing the naked truth; for then the Art would become so easie, that it would be contemned. But what needs words? we know the Truth, and we know by a secret Character, true Writers from Sophisters; and we need no Arguments being eye-witnesses our selves, and know that there is but one truth; nor but one path, even the beaten path in which all who ever have attained this Art have troden, nor can we be deceived our selves; nor would we deceive others.

Did drink the juice of Grapes.

This Toad is said to drink the juice of Grapes according to the Philosopher, the body, saith he, is not nobler than Gold, nor yet the water more pretious than wine. This water they call sometimes *Aqua Ardens*, sometimes *Acetum Acerrimum*, but most commonly they call it their *Mercury*; this denomination I shall not insist upon; but shall assure you that it only deciphers *Mercury*, even that *Mercury*, of which I writ in my little Latine Treatise, called λιθος σοφιας χρυσοποιητικος, or *Introitus apertus ad occlusum Regis palatium*; in that I discovered the whole Truth fully and nakedly, and if not too plainly, I am sure plain enough. I shall not here repeat; to that I remit the Reader.

This juice of Grapes this Toad is said to drink; that is not only in the gross Conjunction, which is an Impastation of the body, with the Water to the temper of *Dough* or *Leaven*, which the Water readily doth: such affinity there is between the Water and the Body; as the Philosopher saith, this Water is friendly and pleasant to the metals. But over, and besides the Water soaks Radically into our Body; being circulated upon it, according as the Philosopher saith, When its own sweat is returned to the Body, it perforates it marvellously. Thus the Body drinks in the Water, or Juice of Grapes, not so much then when they are first mingled: but most especially, when by decoction it pierceth radically to the very profundity of it; and makes it to alter its Form; This is the Water which teareth the Bodies, and makes them no Bodies, but flying Spirits like a Smoak, Wind or Fume, as *Artephius* speaketh plentifully.

This operation is performed in a short while, in comparison of Subterraneal operations of Nature, which are done in a very long time; therefore it is that so many Philosophers say, that it is done in a very short time, and yet it is not without cause, that so many of the Philosophers have complained of the length of this decoction.

Therefore the same *Artephius* who had said, that this fire of the Water of our *Mercury*, doth that in a short time above ground, that Nature was in performing a 1000 years, doth in another place say, that the tincture doth not come out at once, but by little and little each day, and hour, till after along time the decoction be compleat, according to the saying of the Philosopher: Boyl, boyl, and again boyl, and accompt not tedious our long decoction.

So fast.

So then this expression here, that the Toad doth drink in the Juice of Grapes *so fast*, doth not imply but that this work must have the true time of Nature; which is indeed a long time, and so is every decoction at least: so they will seem to the Artist who attends the fire day by day, and yet must wait for the fruit with Patience, till the Heaven have showred down upon the Earth the former and latter Rain: yet be not out of heart, but attend until the compleatment, for then a large Harvest will abundantly recompence all thy toyl.

Till over-charged with the Broth, his Bowels all to brast.

It follows in the Vision, that at length the Toad (over-charged with the broth) did burst asunder; This broth is the same which the fair *Medea* did prepare, and pour upon the two Serpents which did keep the Golden Aples, which grew in the hidden Garden of the Virgins *Hesperides*.

For the Vinegre of the Philosophers being circulated upon the Body, doth engender a substance like unto bloudy Broth, and makes Colours of the Rainbow, to appear in the ascension and descension upon your *Lyon*, until the *Eagles* have at length devoured the *Lyon*, and all together being killed with the Carion of the Carcasses become a venemous Toad, creeping on the Earth, and a Crow swimming in the midst of the dead Sea.

The Juice of Grapes then, which is our *Mercury*, drawn from the Chameleon or Air of our Physical *Magnesia*, and *Chalybs* Magical, being circulated upon our true *Terra Lemnia*; after it is grossly mixed with it by Incorporation, and set to our fire to digest, doth still enter in and upon our Body, and searcheth the profoundity of it; and makes the occult to become manifest by continual ascension and descension: till all together become a Broth; which is a mean substance of dissevered qualities, between the Water and the Body, till at length the Body burst asunder and be reduced into a Powder, like to the Atoms of the Sun, black of the blackest and of a viscous matter.

And after that, from poysoned bulk he cast his venom fell.

This Reduction of the Body, thus in this water ingenders so venomous a Nature, that truly in the whole World there is not a ranker Poyson, or stink, according as Philosophers witness: And therefore he is said to cast his fell venom from his poysoned bulk; in as much as the exhalations are compared to the Invenomed Fume of Dragons, as *Flamell* in his Summary hath such an Allusion. But the Philosopher (as he adds in his *Hieroglyphicks* of the two Dragons,) never feels his stink, unless he break his Vessels, but only he judgeth it by the colours proceeding from the rottenness of the Confections.

And indeed it is a wonder to consider, (which some Sons of Art are eye-witnesses of) that the fixed and most digested Body of Gold; should so rot and putrifie, as if it were a Carcass, which is done by the admirable Divine virtue of our dissolving Water, which no Money can purchase. All these operations, which are so enlarged by variety of expressions, center in one, which is killing the quick, and reviving the dead.

For grief and pain whereof his members all began to swell.

This venemous fume of exhalations returning upon the Body, cause it to swell all over according to the saying of the Philosopher; The Body in this Water puffeth up, swelleth and putrifieth as a Grain of Corn, taking the nature living and vegetable, therefore for this cause this Water is in this sence called by the Philosophers their Leaven, for as Leaven causeth Past[e] to swell, so this fermenteth the body, and causeth it to tumefie and puff up; it is also called venom, for as venom causeth swelling, so this Water by its reiteration uncessantly upon our body.

This operation is uncessant from the first incitation of the matter, even until compleat putrefaction; for the Toad doth always send forth his exhalations (being rather called the *Lyon*,) till he be over-come in part: and then when the Body begins a little to put on the Nature of the Water, and the Water of the Body, then it is compared to two Dragons, one winged, and the other without wings: and lastly when that stinking Earth appears, which *Hermes* calls his *Terra Foliata*, or Earth of Leaves, then it is most properly called the Toad of the Earth; from the first excitation, even to the last of this putrefaction: which exhalations are at the beginning for a time White, and afterwards become Yellowish, Blewish, and Blackish, (from the virulency of the matter) which exhalations hourly condensing, and ever and anon running down like little veins in drops, do enter the Body marvelously, and the more it is entred; the more it swells and puffs up, till at length it be compleatly putrefied.

With drops of poysoned sweat, approaching thus his secret Den.

The following two Verses then are but a more Ample description of this work; of volatization which is an ascension, and descension, or circulation of the confections within the Glass. Which Glass here called the secret Den, is else-where called by the same Author, a little Glassen-tun, and is an ovall Vessel; of the purest White Glass, about the bigness of an ordinary Hen-Egg, in the which about the quantity of an ounce of 8 drachms of the confection, in all mixed is a convenient proportion to be set, which being Seal'd up with *Hermes* Seal, the Glass having a neck about 6 fingers high, or thereabouts, which being thin and narrow; is melted together Artificially, that no Spirits can get out, nor no Air can come in, in which respect it is named a secret Den.

Also it is called a secret Den, because of the secretness of Ashes or Sand, in which in a Philosophical Athanor it is set, the doores being firmly shut up, and a prospect left to look in by a Window, either to open a little, as much as is convenient sometimes, as occasion requires, or else with Glass put into it, to admit the view of the Artist; together with a light at hand to shew the colours.

His Cave with blasts of fumous Air, he all bewhited then.

Which Glass, Nest, and Furnace being thus secretly ordered, the Artist must in the first place expect to be in Prison a long time, as *Bernard Trevisan* saith, for the Concave of this secret place, will be so bewhited with the fumes which ascend, that an Artist rules his work more by skill and reason, or the eye of the mind, then of the Body, for the Spirits arising like a smoak or Wind, sticketh to the Concave of the Glass, which is above the Sand or Ashes, and there by degrees, there grow drops which run down and moisten the Body below, and reduce as much as they can of the fixed, and so the Body by the Water, and the Water by the Body alter their colours.

And from the which in space a Golden Humour did ensue.

Inso much that at length, the whole Vessel will seem as though it were all over gilded with Gold, for the exhalations will be Yellow, which is a sign of true Copulation of our Man & Woman together, but before this Yellow, and with it there will be an obscuring of the White brightness of the Fume, with mixture of Colours, Dark, obscure and Blewish.

The space is not long, for all the several passages are conspicuous before 40 days; for in that space from these Colours, are demonstrating Signs of Corruption and Generation, which is given us by the biting, and fiery Nature of our pontick Waters, and the resistance of our Bodies; in which Fight the Body is over-come, and killed, and dying yields these Colours: which is a Sign that the Eagles now are getting the Mastery, and that our Lyon hath also a little infected them with his Carcass, which they begin to prey upon. This Operation is by Ingenious Artists called Extraction of Natures, and Separation, for the Tincture begins now to be separated from the Body. Also Reduction to the first matter; which is Sperm or Seed, which by reason of its double Nature, is compared to two Dragons. I shall not enlarge in this Vision, but briefly unfold what is briefly laid down.

Whose falling drops from high did stain the soyl with ruddy hue.

These colours of the *Mercury*, do affect the subsident fixed Body, with sutable colours and the Bodies from these exhalations, be Tincted with a ruddy colour, which *Flamel* expresseth to this purpose, that these two Natures, or Dragons do bite one another very cruelly; and never leave from the time they have seised one upon another; till by their slavering Venom, and mortal hurts, they be all of a gore bloud, and then being stewed in their own Venom, are changed into a fifth Essence.

And when his Corps the force of vital breath began to lack.

But before the renovation of these Natures, they must in the first place pass through the Eclipse, both of the Sun and Moon and the darkness of Purgatory, which is the Gate of Blackness, and after that they shall be renovated with the light of Paradise.

This Allegorically is called Death, for as a man will resist violence, which intrencheth upon his life as long as he can, but if his Enemies are many and mighty, at length they grow too mighty for him, and he begins to fail both in strength and courage, and so Paleness, the Harbinger of Death, doth stand as it were on his lips, so our Body or Man the *Sun,* like a strong Champion, doth resist long, till he be wounded, and bleed as it were all over, and then dies, at whose death blackness doth begin to appear, as of old the Ravens were foretellers of Mans death approaching: for this Reiteration of Rotation of the Influences of the Heaven of it, together with Heat still drying up and soaking in the Moisture as fast as it falls, brings it at last naturally to die and corrupt, as any other thing doth.

And then the Corps begin to lack breath; that is, the Fumes begin to cease: for with oft ascending and descending the Spirits are somewhat fixed, and turned into Powder or Dust, and are now in the bottom of the Vessel, drawing fast to Putrefaction: Nor do they for a time ascend, but remain below.

Wherefore govern your Fire, that your Spirits be not so exalted, and climb so high that the Earth want them, and they return no more: For this Operation is, as *Morien* saith, a drawing out of Water from the Earth, and again a returning of the same to the Earth, so often and so long till the Earth putrefie.

This dying Toad became forthwith like Coal for colour black.

This is the final end of the Combat, for herein in this Earth of Leaves all are reconciled, and final Peace is made; and now one Nature embraceth another, in no other form but in the form of a Powder impalpable, and in no other colour but black of the blackest.

From henceforth Natures are united, and boil and bubble together like melted Pitch, and change their forms one into another. Take heed therefore lest instead of Powder Black of the Blackest, which is the Crows Bill, you have an unprofitable dry half red Precipitate, Orange-coloured, which is a certain sign of the Combustion of Flowers, or Vertue of the Vegetative Seed. On this very Rock I have stumbled, and do therefore warn you.

Thus drowned in his proper Veins of poysoned Flood.

It appears by all that hath been said, and by the undoubted Testimony of all Philosophers who have been Eye-witnesses to this Truth, that the work is not so tedious, nor so chargeable, but that in the simple way of Nature the Mastery is to be attained: for when once the true body is Impasted with its true Leven, it doth calcine it self, and dissolve it self for the dissolution of the Body into a black and changeable coloured Water, which is the sign of egression of the Tincture, is the Congelation of the Spirits into this lowest Period of Obscurity, which is this black Powder like unto Lamp-Black, this is the Complement of Eclipsation, which Contrition begins soon after the Colours, Yellowish, Blewish, &c.

For term of Eighty Days and Four he rotting stood.

This Calcination begins with these Variations in Colour about the two and fortieth day, or fiftieth at the farthest, in a good Regimen: After which comes putrefying Corruption, like to the Scum of boiling bloody Broath or melted Pitch; but Blackness in part, *to wit, Superficial,* begins about the fortieth day after the stirring up of the matter, in case of right Progress and Regimen of the Fire, or about the fiftieth at farthest. But this drowning of him in his own Poyson, and stewing him in his own Broath, is the intire Blackness and Cimmerian utter Darkness of compleat Rottenness, which according to the Author, is for the space of eighty four days. This time is not certainly agreed upon by Authors: But in this they all agree, they prescribe so long time until the Complement. One writes, *That this Blackest Black indures a long time, and is not destroyed in less than five months.* Another writes, *That the King when he enters into his Bath pulls off his Robe, and gives it to* Saturn, *from whom he receives a Black Shirt, which he keeps forty two days:* And indeed it is two and forty days before he put on this Black Shirt instead of his Golden Robe, that is, be destroyed as touching his Solary Qualities, and become instead of Fixt, Citrine, Terrene, and Solid, a Fugitive, Black, Spiritual, Watery, and Flegmatick Substance: But Putridness begins not till the first Forms be put off; for so long as the Body may be reduced into its former Nature, it is not yet well ground and imbibed: grind therefore and imbibe, till thou see the Bodies to become no Bodies, but a Fume and Wind, and then circulating for a season, thou shalt see them settle and putrifie.

    Saturn then will hold the Earth, which is Occidental, Retentive and Autumnal, in the West; then proceed to the North, where *Mercury* holdeth the Water, where the Matter is Watery and Flegmatick, and it is Winter, and the North expulsive. But they who divide the Operation into *Saturn*'s Rule, and after him succeeding *Jupiter,* ascribe to *Saturn* the whole of Putridness, and to *Jupiter* the time of variety of Colours. After *Jupiter,* who holds but twenty or two and twenty days, comes *Luna,* the third Person, bright and fair, and she holds twenty good days, sometimes two over and above: In this Computation it is good to count from the fortieth or fiftieth day of the first beginning of the Stone, to the fourteenth or sixteenth day of *Jupiter*'s Reign, wherein in the washing of *Laton* there is still Blackness, though mixed with variety of gay Colours, which amounteth to the sum of days allowed by the Author in Putrifaction, to wit, Eighty four days. Accounting intire Blackness, with *Augurellus,* after four times eleven days and nights, which make four and forty: Or, according to another Philosopher, which saith, *In the first Fifty Days there appears the True Crow, and after it in Threescore and Ten Dayes the White Dove; and after in Fourscore and Ten Days the Tyrian Colour.*

By Tryal then this Venom to expel I did desire;
For which I did commit his Carcass to a gentle Fire.
Which done, a Wonder to the sight, but more to be rehearst;
The Toad with Colours rare through every side was pierc'd.
And white appear'd when all the sundry hews were past;
Which after being tincted, ruddy for evermore did last.

I shall add my own Sentence: Mix thy two Natures well, and if thy matter be pure, both the Body, and the Water, and the internal Heat of thy Bath as it ought to be, and the external Fire gentle, and not violent; yet so that the Matter may circulate, the Spiritual Nature on the Corporal, in six and forty or fifty days expect the beginning of intire Blackness; and after six and fifty days more, or sixty, expect the Peacocks Tayl, and Colours of the Rainbow; and after two and twenty days more, or four and twenty, expect *Luna* perfect, the Whitest White, which will grow more and more glorious for the space of twenty days, or two and twenty at the most: After which, in a little more increased Fire, expect the Rule of *Venus* for the space of forty days, or two and forty; and after it the Rule of *Mars* two and forty days more; and after him the Rule of *Sol flavus* forty days, or two and forty: And then in a moment comes the Tyrian Colour, the sparkling Red, the fiery Vermilion, and Red Poppy of the Rock.

Then of the Venom handled thus a Medicine I did make,
Which Venom kills, and saveth such as Venom chance to take.

Thus onely by Decoction these Natures are changed and altered so wonderfully to this blessed Tincture, which expelleth all Poyson, though it self were a deadly Poyson before the Preparation, yet after it is the Balsam of Nature, expelling all Diseases, and cutting them off as it were with one Hook, all that are accidental to Humane frail Body, which is wonderful.

Glory be to Him the Grantor of such secret Ways;
Dominion and Honour both, with Worship and with Praise.   Amen.

Now GOD only is the Dispenser of these glorious Mysteries: I have been a true Witness of Nature unto thee, and I know that I write true, and all Sons of Art shall by my Writings know that I am a Fellow-Heir with them of this Divine Skill. To the Ignorant I have wrote so plain as may be, and more I had written if the Creator of all things had given me larger Commission. Now to Him alone, as is due, be all Honour, and Power, and Glory, who made all things, and giveth knowledge to whom he listeth of his Servants, and conceals where he pleaseth: To Him be ascribed, as due is, all Service and Honour. And now, Brother, whoever enjoyeth this rare Blessing of God, improve all thy strength to do him service with it, for he is worthy of it, who hath created all things, and for whose sake they were and are created.

The End of Sir George Ripley's *Vision,*
Canon of Bridlington.

The Plates

(Note. The dates given for the manuscripts reproduced here are not those of the original texts they contain.)

1 Ouroboros, the dragon feeding on its own tail, is an emblem of the eternal, cyclic nature of the universe ('from the One to the One'). Here as in all alchemical art the colouring is part of the message: green is the colour of the beginning; red is associated with the goal of the Great Work.

Copy of Synosius by Theodoros Pelecanos, 1478, Bibliothèque Nationale, Paris, Ms. grec 2327, f.297.

ΤΟῦ τε ἐστὶ τὸ μύση
αὐτοῦ. Τοῦτε ἐστὶ
... των τῆς
αὐτοῦ·—

Τὰ δὲ
... αύ
Τό δὲ
Τέ
Τοῦ
Οἱ δὲ
... αυ
σὺν θέ
αὐτοῦ·—
... ἡ τί αὐτοῦ
θε ... καὶ ... οἱ σα

ρίον ὁ οὐροβόρος δράκων·
ἡ λέ ... ὠς τῶν σω
ερ ... ας

τέχνης

τοῦ
ος.

... ἡ τε
τοῦ

φῶτα τῶν ... σηρίων τῆς
ἐστὶ ταῦτα ἢ ἐὰν θωσι·—
... γον αὐτοῦ ἐστὶν ἰω ...
... ἡ ... ψας αὐτοῦ·—
... δὲ ... αὐτοῦ οἱ τέσσαρες ... αἱ
... σωμα τῆς ... τέχνης

αὐτοῦ τοῦτε ἐστὶν τὸ ὁ·

Δράκων τίς ἐστι παρὰ καὶ ταισ φυλάττων τοῦ ναοῦ τοῦτον
τοῦ χειρωσάμενον· πρῶτον θῦσον καὶ ἀπόδειραι τὸ
τοσον, καὶ λαβὼν τὰς σάρκας αὐτοῦ ἕως τῶν ὀστέων,
πρὸς τὸ στόμιον τοῦ ναοῦ ποίησον αὐτὸ βάσις
καὶ ἀναβὰς ἐπὶ τι καὶ εὑρίσκεις ἐκεῖ τὸ ζητούμενον χρῆ
μα. Τοῦτο γὰρ ἱερεὸν τὸν χαλκάνου μετετέθη τοῦ
χρώματος τῆς φύσεως καὶ γέγονεν ἀργύρανον·
ὃν μετ’ ὀλίγασ ὡ ... ἡμέρασ ἐὰν θελήσῃς εὑρί
σεις αὐτόν καὶ χρυσάνον·— ὦ εἰ τοῦ θ(εο)ῦ ἀκαλυπτ

λαβὼν θεῖον ἄπυρον λέιωσον οὔρῳ ἀφθόρου· ᾖτα
λαβὼν ἅλμην δ΄ναί αν ἔψε ἕως ... πλεύσῃ καὶ γί
νεται ἄκαυστον· δοκίμαζον καὶ ἐπὶ τὸ ἕτερον καὶ βλέπων

2 The sign of Aries corresponds to the name of the Materia Prima or subject of the Work. The grey wolf (antimony), devouring Mercury, indicates that a purification of the subject, similar to that of gold by antimony, must take place.

3 A threefold sublimation by means of the secret fire effectively reduces the subject to its root or radical state.

Speculum veritatis, 17th century, Biblioteca Apostolica Vaticana, Cod. lat. 7286, f. 2, 3.

3

overleaf 4 The androgyne represents the conjunction of opposites – a cosmic principle exemplified and symbolized, in Eastern and Western thought alike, by eroticism. Birds, commonly blue eagles, are used by alchemists to refer to the successive volatilizations or sublimations which take place in the Work; here the rising eagle which lifts the androgyne, and the dead eagles beneath its feet, imply, respectively, the volatilization of the fixed and the fixation of the volatile.

5 This enigmatic creature can only represent the harmony which underlies 'our chaos', the Materia Prima. Its heads, limbs and tail show various conjunctions of the Four Elements, and of heat and cold, wet and dry, volatile and fixed.

Aurora consurgens, late 14th century, Zentralbibliothek, Zürich, Cod. rhenovacensis 172, endpapers.

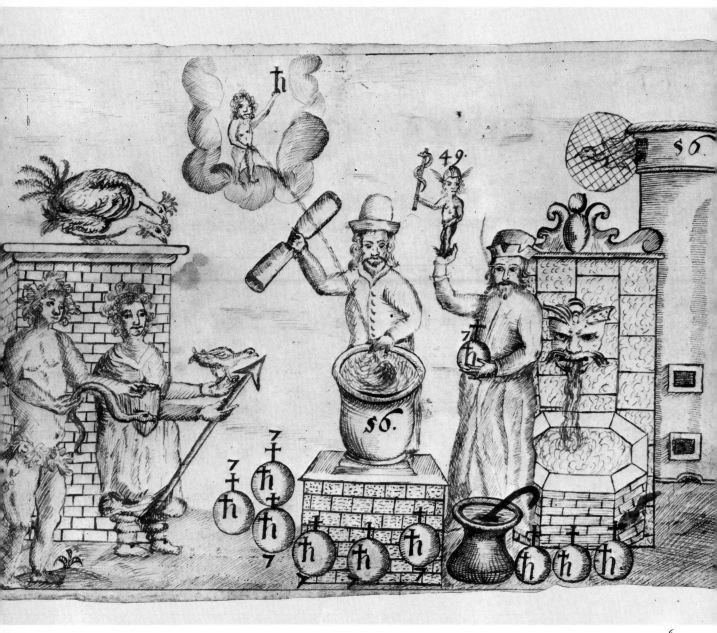

6 Here the Conjunction of Natures prepares for
the separation of light from dark, the emergence
of white from black, which is the birth of Mercury.

7 Vulcan, the secret fire, induces the birds to fly:
which indicates that seven sublimations take place.
The hens indicate the degrees of fire (the heat
which hatches the Philosophic Egg, or alchemical
vessel), and Mercury becomes the Hermaphrodite.

Speculum veritatis, 17th century, Biblioteca Apostolica Vaticana, Cod. lat. 7286, f. 4, 5.

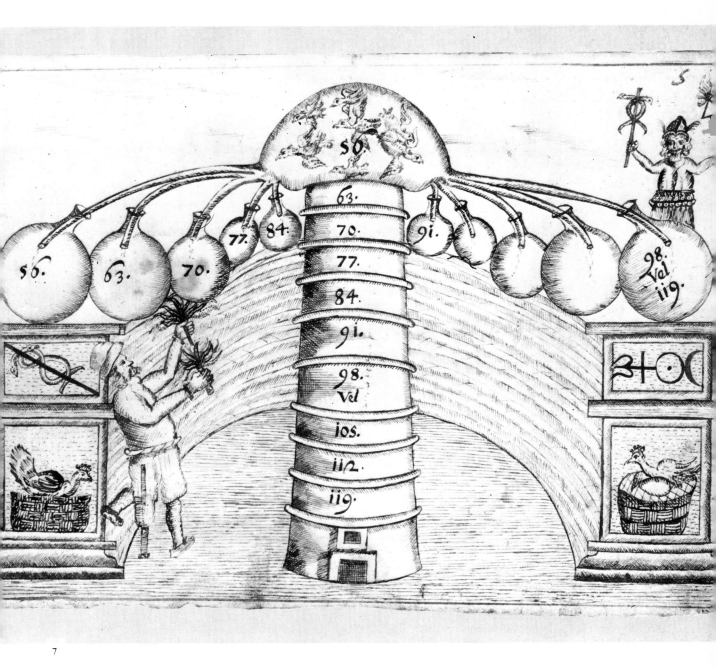

7

overleaf 8 This illustration of successive stages of the 'subtile Werk' shows the master preparing ingredients. One worker separates 'earth from fire and the subtle from the gross', and another, in the course of repeated distillations in a vessel called a pelican, witnesses the transitional stage called the Peacock's Tail, in which iridescent colours appear (see Iris, pl. 57).

9 Four of the great alchemists preside over the Work: Geber, Arnold of Villanova, Rhasis and Hermes Trismegistus. The worker on the left is pounding the raw subject in a mortar; those in the middle are seeing to it that it repeatedly absorbs its own distilled moisture; and the one on the right, under the auspices of Hermes, is repeatedly 'cooking the white' (*albedo*) until it germinates.

Norton's Ordinall, 15th century, British Museum, London, Add. 10.302, f. 37v., 32v.

ye may not w metalle or qwyk sylver be gynn
To make Elixer if ye entende to wynn
yett if ye destroye there hole composicion
Som of there copmnents wil help i 2 dilion
And that is nothing els of y con or that odre
But only magnesia & litarge hir broder

10

10 The philosophers venerate their prepared Mercury. Some, but not all, offer him gold.

11 Here 'our mercury' is freed from outer impurities. This is an example of a common trap set by alchemists to confuse the unwary: the beginning of the Work is placed here half-way through a twelve-picture sequence.

Speculum veritatis, 17th century, Biblioteca Apostolica Vaticana, Cod. lat. 7286, f. 6, 7.

11

overleaf 12 An Arab alchemist, Senior Zadith, consults the Tables of Hermes. Before him the Elixir is displayed. The archer eagles are an elegant conjunction of opposites. The eagles (see pls. 4, 7), which vary in number according to different sources, signify successive sublimations; the bows and arrows mean fixation, as well as possessing an astrological significance (Sagittarius).

13 Here Sun and Moon, male and female, fixed and volatile, the sulphur and mercury of the philosophers, do battle. The encounter of opposites can also be seen as sexual (see pls. 4, 37, 38). In alchemy, as in the Tao doctrine of Yin and Yang, each opposing principle contains its opposite: hence the shields.

14 Here the green (raw) subject is overcome and fixed by an antithetical pair: the solar and lunar warriors in slightly different guise. Here they are said to be its 'brother and sister', without whom it can never germinate and become the Philosophers' Stone. The sister, alias Diana, has the black skin of the *nigredo* and the white garment of the *albedo*.

Aurora consurgens, late 14th century, Zentralbibliothek, Zürich, Cod. rhenovacensis 172, f. 3, 10, 36.

tant Qui habet aures audiendi audi
at / quid dicat spus doctrine / filie discipline
de spu septiformis virtute / quo omnes myslet spu
turn / qd plu insinuant his verbis / Distilla
septies / et separari ab humid corrumpente

Ce De domo thaurina quia sapia fundauit   sup petrum
·c· 10·

Sapiencia edificauit sibi domum / quia q̈s
introierit saluabit / et pastua inueiet
teste ipa Inebriabut ab uber Domus
tue / qz melior e dies vna in atriis eius / sup
milia / O qum bti qui hitant in domo har / In
ea namq qui petit accipit / et qui querit inue
nit set pulsanti apietur / Nam sapia stat ad

Chiramen petit id qd petit omeb hijs figuris
Et inues ego dicol Genie in scriptura

nat vngendo / dicut n· phn / cp si dat?ms sint
de eo m aqua nl vino tepido palit?ff srene

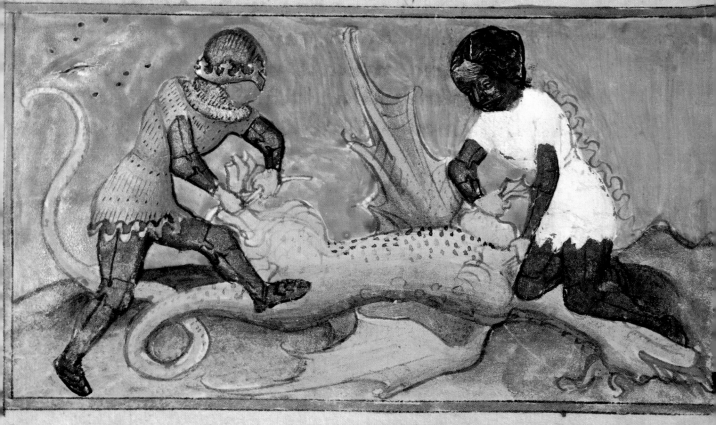

15 The vessel or Philosophic Egg is here entrusted to the care of Vulcan (see pl. 7), so that the chicken of the wise may hatch.

16 *Solve et coagula* (see p. 16); Mercury transfixes the king, and the fixed is thus made volatile; while Cadmus or sulphur fixes the volatile by transfixing the serpent. Cadmus, in Greek mythology, killed the serpent that guarded the Castalian Spring, and sowed its teeth, which came up armed men.

Speculum veritatis, 17th century, Biblioteca Apostolica Vaticana, Cod. lat. 7286, f. 8, 9.

16

overleaf 17 All the Graeco-Roman myths carry an alchemical interpretation. Here, as in Book VI of Vergil's *Aeneid,* Aeneas takes the Golden Bough which will enable him to pass unscathed through Hell (as the subject passes through the fire and lives). The tree is the alchemical Tree of Life; the three figures (showing three generations of Aeneas' family, Silvius, Aeneas and Anchises) wear the alchemical livery of black, white and red; the birds of sublimation wheel overhead. The white-headed raven signifies that the black (*nigredo*) yields up the white.

Salomon Trismosin, *Splendor solis,* 16th century, British Museum, London, Harley 3469.

18 Twin fountains signify the two waters which (in an alchemical sense) are sulphurous (red) and mercurial (white). These are united by a unifying principle (the Knight), who wields a sword (the secret fire). The colours of his armour – black, white, transitional yellow, red and gold – summarize the Work.

Salomon Trismosin, *La Toyson d'or* [a later version of *Splendor solis*], 18th century, Bibliothèque Nationale, Paris, Ms. français 12.297, f. 14.

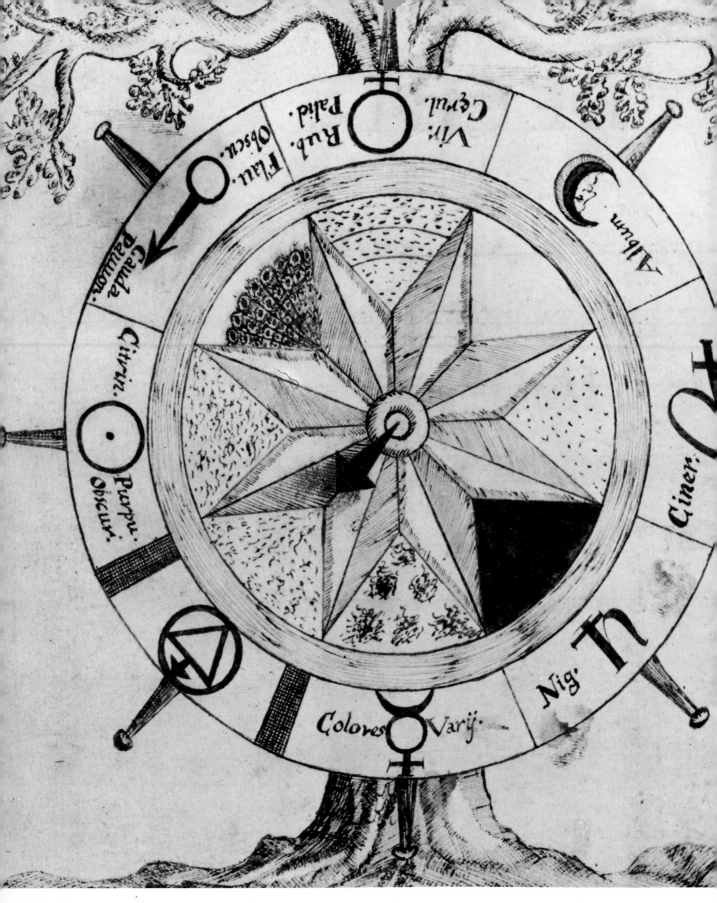

19 Cadmus (see pl. 16) spins the wheel of the Work, and thus reiterates all its operations. With 'our sulphur', he nails the first nail – which means that he fixes the volatile matter, by causing it to be digested together with the fixed. Digestion is synonymous with the whole sequence of operations known as distillation, sublimation, imbibation, ceration, solution, coagulation, etc.

Speculum veritatis, 17th century, Biblioteca Apostolica Vaticana, Cod. lat. 7286, f. 10.

overleaf

20 The green lion, in the illustrations of the *Rosarium,* is often supposed to be eating the Sun; but the blood suggests a likelier interpretation. The lion's colour shows it to be matter in a green, raw, primordial state, from which the sulphurous and mercurial principles are extracted. The 'blood of the green lion', in alchemical lore, is the Hermetic Mercury, which it disgorges together with the Sun (the Sulphur of the Wise).

21 The crown of perfection rests on the hermaphrodite's head; the fixed and the volatile are now for ever united. The hydra in the cup effectively symbolizes the Elixir and its triple dominion over the three realms of nature, while the single snake suggests the Unity which is born from the Trinity. The three-headed dragon is there as a reminder that the success of the Work rests on a three-fold solution. The pelican symbolizes the cyclic distillation and alludes to the Exaltation of the Quintessence.
Rosarium philosophorum, 16th century, Stadt-bibliothek Vadiana, St Gallen, Ms. 394 a, f. 97, 92.

perfeccionis ostensio

22 After a threefold rotation of the wheel (the three works or sequences of operations which make up the Work), and after a renewed fermentation and nutrition, the nature of the Elixir, the Son of the Sun, born from the Philosophic Egg, is fixed with a triple nail.

23 The kings of the earth worship the Perfect Red King, or sulphur of the philosophers, Shining Lord of the Three Realms.

24 Once multiplied in quantity and quality, the Elixir shows its virtues by transmuting the 'terrestrial planets' or earthly metals. The multiplication is achieved when the Work is performed all over again using the Exalted Matter as the subject instead of the raw *Materia Prima*. See pl. 3, which refers to this part of the Work.

Speculum veritatis, 17th century, Biblioteca Apostolica Vaticana, Cod. lat. 7286, f. 11, 12, 13.

overleaf 25, 26 The root of all things is green, says the Arab philosopher Haly. This is the prepared raw subject, unripe yet ready to progress. The seven green poppies will eventually become one golden bloom, as in the right-hand picture. Here the redness of the King's robe is the sign of the state of perfect fixation and fixed perfection which is known as the Red Rose (see also pl. 63, pp. 118–19).

Johannes Andreae, 15th century, British Museum, London, Sloane 2560, f. 5, 15.

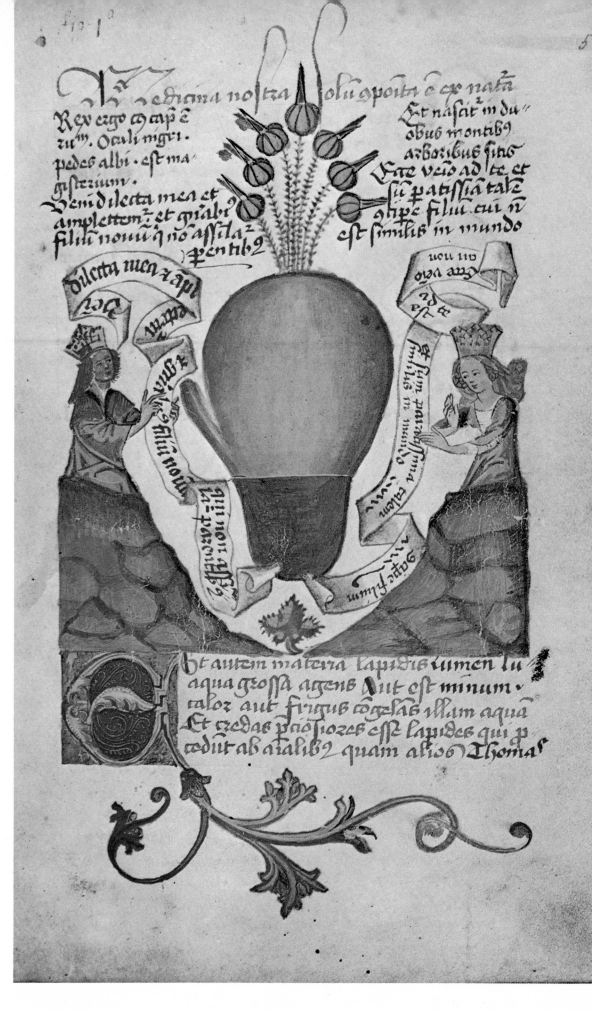

Rosa Rubea

Elix rubeū

R sine exibit tibi rex suo dyademate coro
natus fulgens vt sol clarus vt carbūculus
foris effluens vt cera · pseuerās in igne ·
penetrās et retinens argentū vivum Ar
color namqz rubedinis causat noldus
ex cōplemento digestionis · dm sanguis
non generatur in homine nisi pirq diligeter
coquatur in epate · sicut nos cum videmus vriñz
de mane vrina alba · facntes parz dorū

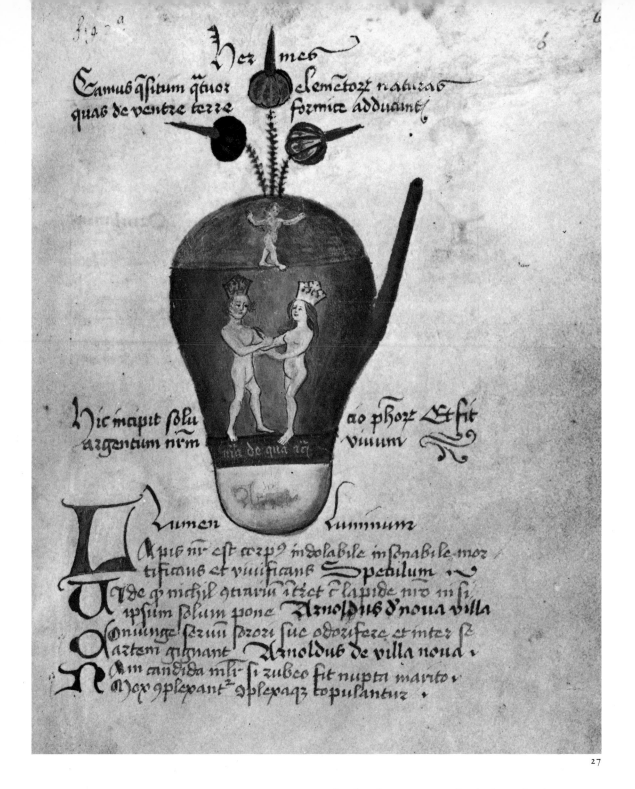

27 In the first process of solution, the king and queen (see note to pls. 25–26) remove the impurities from each other until they stand naked.

28 Conjunction or perfect solution: the two bodies are made one as they dissolve into the liquid state.

Johannes Andreae, 15th century, British Museum, London, Sloane 2560, f. 6,7.

overleaf 29 The manuscript from which pls. 29–34 and 46 are taken, the so-called *Nozze*, reads as an account of a historical wedding attended with an exceptional amount of pageantry; but its illustrations show it to be something more. These are alchemical nuptials; and among the guests are the planetary gods of antiquity. The two Negro pages shown here show the black yielding up the white (compare the symbolic raven in pl. 17); the white ferment or seed always precedes the red, which is still concealed (the other basket). The spear is the secret fire (also variously shown as a sword, an arrow, or the club of Hercules).

30 The male principle, the 'seed' at the beginning of the Work, is sometimes called the Old Man. Here, in the bowels of the earth, he weds the female principle; at the summit stands a beckoning angel (volatile) in a red castle (fixed). The alchemists refer to this old man as Boaz, the farmer of Bethlehem whose bride was Ruth the gleaner.

Nicola d'Antonio degli Agli, 1480, Biblioteca Apostolica Vaticana, Cod. Urb. lat. 899, f. 106 v., 91.

dui grandissimi cisti doro pieni &
colmi di uarie confectioni· Et in
meço del camello era un garçone
ethiope negro che mettendo ambe
dui le mani aluna mo allaltra di
queste ceste spargeua & gittaua dic
ti confetti al populo pertutta lasala
& che era bellissima & mirabil cosa
ad uedere·

31

31 The seven planetary gods are associated with metals (the 'terrestrial planets'). But these links are not always to be taken at face value. Thus, the Moon here is not 'vulgar' silver. Her horns and arrow refer to the secret fire. 'Diana naked' is the water which washes the *nigredo*.

Mercury one day cast his staff down on two fighting snakes, and they coiled round it to produce his emblem, the caduceus, symbol of the harmonious conjunction of opposites.

32 Mars holds a gold-handled. red-sheathed dagger and a silver and gold sword; his scarf is white. He is thus not vulgar iron but the subject passing through the reign of Mars, i.e. approaching a certain degree of perfection.

Jupiter (whose vulgar metal is tin) is often likened to the natural heat which generates all things; he dwells in the sky, and the earth is the place of his pleasures.

32

BIBLIOTECA APOSTOLICA VATICANA

overleaf 33, 34 Venus and vulgar copper share a symbol; but here, with her winged helmet of volatility and the arrow of the secret fire, she represents the mercurial, white, female element in the drama of the Great Work. It bears within it (pl. 13) its opposing principle; and so her undergarment is masculine, sulphurous red.

The Philosophers' Stone is said to be attained through a conjunction of Sol and Luna in the sign of Leo. Sol here is not gold but the red sulphur of the philosophers (pls. 23, 26). Note his triple whip and reins, signifying dominion over the three realms, animal, vegetable and mineral.

Nicola d'Antonio degli Agli, 1480, Biblioteca Apostolica Vaticana, Cod. Urb. lat. 899, f. 97, 99, 98.

VENVS

·SOL·

35 Alchemists use the Judgment of Paris to refer to the end of the First Work, a fixation of the volatile; the making of the Stone is thus the siege of Troy, and that of the Elixir is its fall.

36 Fire and Water are united through their qualities, heat and moisture; this union takes place in Air, and is achieved by Mercury.

De Alchimia, 16th c., Bibliotheek der Rijksuniversiteit, Leiden, Cod. Voss. chem. f29, f. 78, 89.

overleaf 37, 38 There is only one process of solution, says Pernety; but it takes many forms. The *Donum Dei* shows, within the outline of the Philosophic Egg, a number of these conjunctions of opposites. Perfect solution is the moment in the First Work (pl. 28) in which the solid is dissolved by the volatile spirit within it (see the neck of the glass), and unites with the liquid or volatile contents of the vessel.

In putrefaction the couple dissolve in the black *nigredo*; no generation without corruption. They pass through death to produce a perfect child.

Pretiosissimum Donum Dei [*per*] *Georgium Anrach*, 17th century, Bibliothèque de l'Arsenal, Paris, Ms. 975, f. 13, 14.

F. SOLVTIO PERFECTA III.

Aqua

39 From death comes new life. While the body remains below, the volatile part rises, just as the human soul and spirit leave the body when death releases them.

40 No generation without corruption; no life without death (see pls. 31, 38). The blackness of putrefaction must precede the whiteness, as night precedes day.

Anon., 14th century, Biblioteca Mediceo-Laurenziana, Florence, Ms. Ashburn 1166, f. 16, 17v.

overleaf 41, 42 Here again, as in pl. 37, the lovers represent the perfect solution of the (solar and lunar) opposites in the first water – the central event of the First Work (left).

In the Second Work, the conjunction is repeated, with the two bodies in a volatile state (hence the wings); this is what is known as the fermentation.

Rosarium philosophorum, 16th century, Stadtbibliothek Vadiana, St Gallen, Ms. 394a, f. 34, 64.

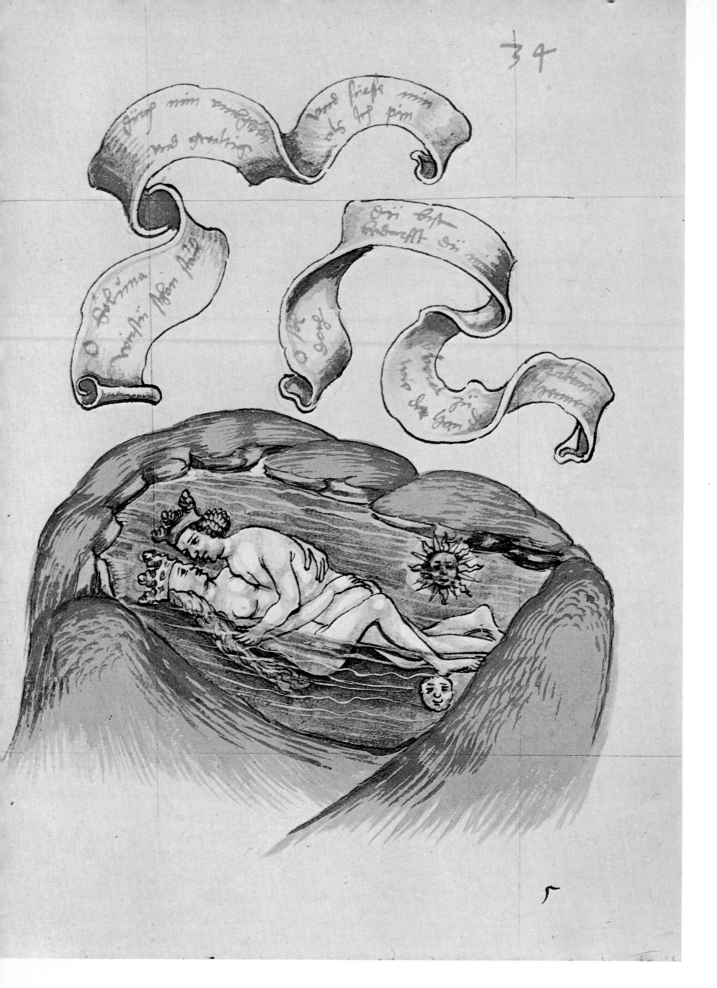

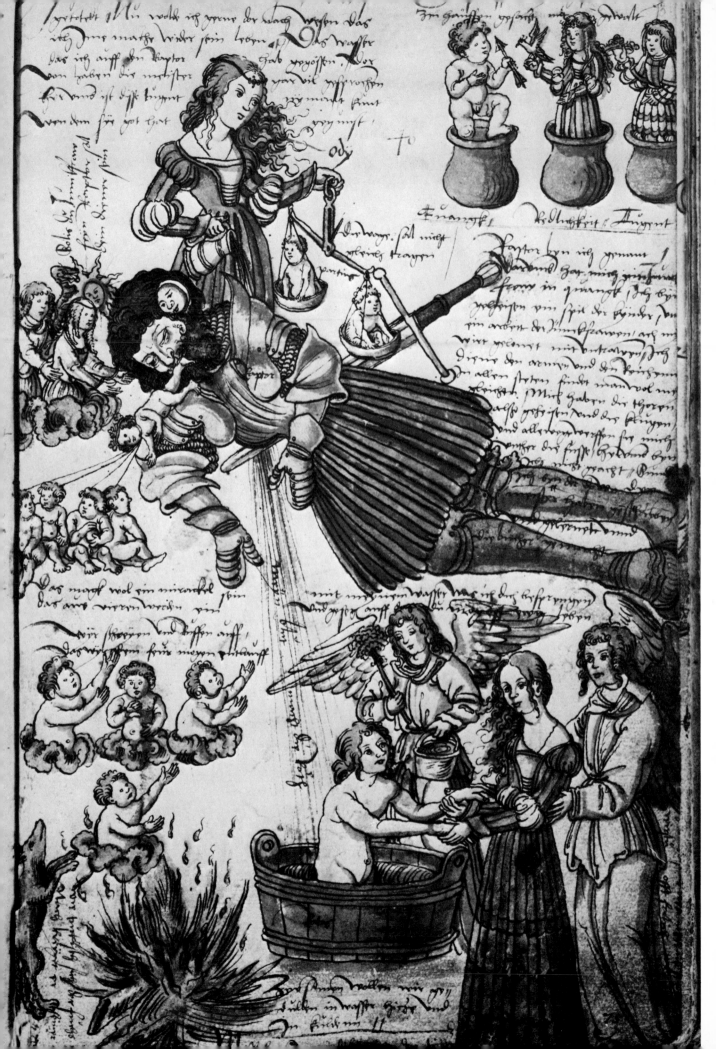

Pan siluanus

44

43 Saturn yields up the children that he has swallowed (see pl. 58). He is the lead of the wise, which is the Materia Prima, imbibed and heated in the right proportions; there is, says Senior, a living thing that is no longer mortal once it has been confirmed and assured of life by means of an eternal and continuous multiplication (pl. 24).

De Alchimia, 16th c., Bibliotheek der Rijksuniversiteit, Leiden, Cod. Voss. chem. f29, f. 73.

44 Pan is the son of Mercury; his head and body form the hieroglyph of the mercury of the philosophers (p. 126), at once solar and lunar. The star on the right is the hieroglyph of the harmoniac salt, the third component of the Art (which is often called the Art of Music).

Anon., 14th century, Biblioteca Mediceo-Laurenziana, Florence, Ms. Ashburn 1166, f.18.

overleaf 45 Mount Helicon is the home of the nine Muses. Crowned, the Old Man (see pl. 30) is surrounded by the Muses, who are the handmaidens of Apollo or Sol (pl. 34), and who personify purity and harmony. On the mountain are the Tree of Life and the twin fountains (pls. 17, 18).

Nicola d'Antonio degli Agli, 1480, Biblioteca Apostolica Vaticana, Cod. Urb. lat. 899, f. 110v.

46 The female principle has in mythology a destructive as well as a creative aspect; thus, Muses create, Sirens destroy. Sirens or mermaids lure sailors to a watery grave, as the mercury of the wise (pl. 22) drowns its solid counterpart. Note the colours of the Work (green, black, white, red, gold), and the emblems of the Elements.

Solidonius, 18th century, Bibliothèque de L'Arsenal, Paris, Ms. 973, f. 12.

Vogliamo ancor de suoi libretti ornate
Chesono de eloquentia larghi fiumi
Riceue adunq̃ sue sublime carte
Et fa che anostri studij sia benigna
Cum opra & cum ingegni in omni parte
Accio che di maior ti facci degna

MONS. ELICON.

ASTRONOMIA
RETTORICA.
GRAMATICA.

Figura II.

SA TVR NVS.

Collatione gra... nde del... Lunedi aoe:

Aucua el præfato Signor Misser Constantio
per prima facto fare gran numero di Castelli di çucharo con tori merli, spiritelli, arme,
arbori, fiori, animali, & altre cose tucte di çuca-
ro: de erano lauorati ad oro, & coloti fini grādi
& larghi quanto potea pōtare uno homo. & olā
de questi castelli molti uafi allanticha. & aquile
& lioni & altri animali di çuchero tutti boni da
māgiare pieni de bandirole doro: & hauea or-
dinato ottanta gioueni equali: liquali haueano
gonellini cutti ameça cofta di tela dorata. &
frappata tō le mani ch fino admezo braccio alla fran-

47 In another image from the sequence of planetary gods (pls. 29–34), Saturn, holding the sickle which is his customary attribute, represents the lead of the wise (see pls. 43, 58).

Nicola d'Antonio degli Agli, 1480, Biblioteca Apostolica Vaticana, Cod. Urb. lat. 8999, f. 99.

48 The mercury of the philosophers (see pls. 22, 44); the *Turba*, from which this image comes, is a classic text in which the philosophers of antiquity engage in a debate on the nature of the world and of matter.

Turba philosophorum, 16th century, Bibliothèque Nationale, Paris, Ms. lat. 7171, f. 16.

48

overleaf 49, 50 A corollary of the belief in the Four Elements has always been the existence of a fifth, Ether or Quintessence. Here it is derived from the Elements (the ring) by alchemical means (the pelican), and exalted or perfected (the second circular symbol, enclosing the phoenix rising from the flames). 'This perfection', we are told, 'is not obtained through the operations of vulgar chemistry but by a simple digestion with the help of the philosophical fire.'

Sapientia veterum philosophorum sive doctrina eorundem de summa et universali medicina, 18th c., Bibliothèque de l'Arsenal, Paris, Ms. 974, fig. xxxvii, xxxviii (see p. 108ff.).

Figura XXXVII.

EXALTATIO V.ˣ ESSENTIÆ

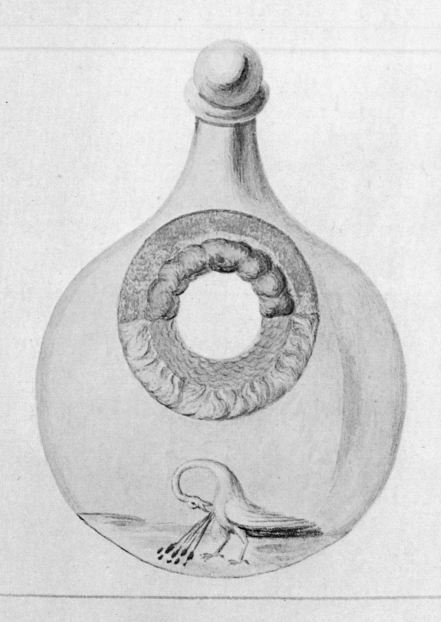

4

Figura XXXVIII.

V.ª Essentia Exaltata

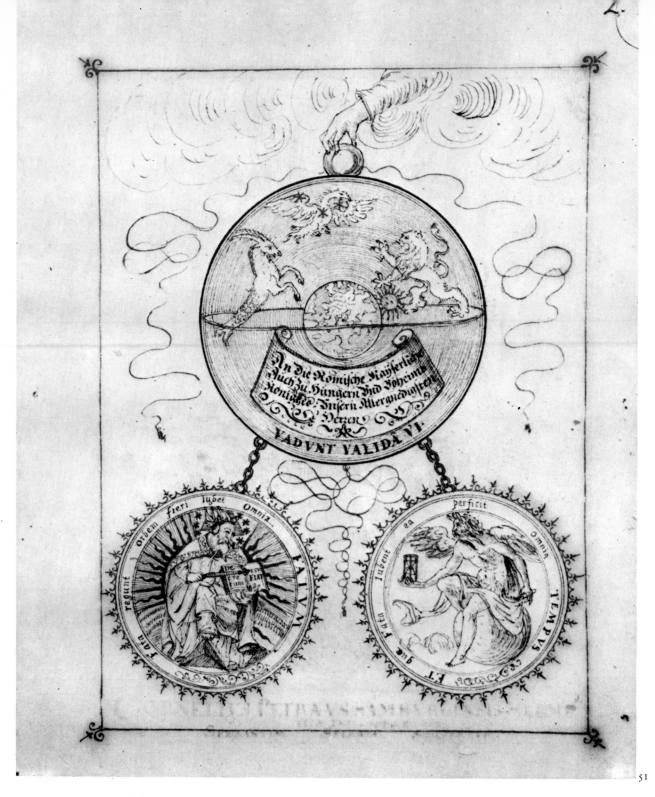

51 The macrocosmic triad of World, Fate and Time is held in equilibrium by the hand of God, and reflected on the microcosmic level by the alchemical triad of Lion, Eagle and Capricorn.

52 A Hermetic philosopher's *ex-libris* or bookplate. On the shield, Mercury is borne down on one side by a heavy weight (fixation) and borne up on the other side by his wings (volatilization).

Sylva philosophorum, 17th century, Bibliotheek der Rijksuniversiteit, Leiden, Cod. Voss. chem. q. 61, f. 2, 3.

CORNELIVS PETRÆVS·HAMBVRGENSIS·HERME,
TICÆ PHILOSOPHIÆ STVD:
SPERANTEM SPERATA SEQVVNTVR.

52

overleaf 53 The nine Muses are seen here with their patron Apollo, who is sitting in his chariot and holding his bow and the arrow of the secret fire. The red colour (pl. 34) indicates the sulphur of the philosophers; the raven, the *nigredo*. The Tree of Life (in the chariot) is frequently associated with Apollo.

54 It is likely that the king's nakedness and whiteness, and the horns on his head, refer to the operation of calcination or purification, which is associated with the Zodiacal sign of Aries the Ram (see note to pl. 2). The woman is wearing a red cloak trimmed with grey, the colour of Jupiter; her belt is black, the colour of Saturn. The subject is emerging from the black shadow of death, hence his victorious crown. The Harpies, offspring of Earth and Sea, were as deadly as their cousins the Sirens (pl. 46); their sister was Iris (pl. 57).

Anon., 15th century, Biblioteca Apostolica Vaticana, Cod. Pal. lat. 1066, f. 218v., 222v.

55

55 The frequent alchemical references to death, burial and rebirth mean that the subject is sealed inside the Egg to decay and be reborn in glory. The philosophers have often depicted the life of Christ in this esoteric light.

56 The Green King must die. The hideous Stymphalides (death-bringers, like the Harpies in pl. 54) are summoning him, and the Three Fates are about to end his life; Atropos cuts the thread spun by Clotho and measured by Lachesis. This king represents the root, the primordial source from which all things grow.

56

overleaf 57 The lady is Iris, the rainbow, Juno's messenger and the harbinger of death to women, as Mercury is to men. To release the souls of women, in alchemy, means to sublime the volatile parts of the residue after the *nigredo*, thus producing the rainbow colouring which is called the Peacock's Tail.

58 Saturn holds a sickle; Rhea a stone. He had castrated and deposed his father Uranus; and to avoid the same fate, ate all his own children. Once Rhea substituted a stone; and the child, Jupiter, grew up to castrate and depose his father. Myths of this kind reflect the cyclic nature of the Great Work.

Anon., 15th century, Biblioteca Apostolica Vaticana, Cod. Pal. lat. 1066, f. 218, 221, 223, 226.

59

59 Here, again, the king is about to meet his doom (see notes to pls. 55, 56). The eight eagles symbolize repeated sublimations. In his left hand the king holds the orb, which is a hieroglyph of the name of the subject, corresponding to the celestial sign of Aries. In this sense the death alluded to is a fixation of the volatile, whereby Water becomes Earth.

60 Mercury kills (or fixes) Argus, the hundred-eyed guardian. Argus' charge, the cow Io, was said by the Greeks to change colour with the phases of the Moon: black, white and red. It was Argus' eyes that went to decorate the peacock's tail (see pl. 57). The weaponry alludes, as always, to the secret fire.

60

overleaf 61 In a castle which represents the philosopher's furnace, Lady Alchimia (see pl. 22) dwells in state with her consort the Athanor King. In accordance with the maxim 'no generation without corruption', she carries a shield with the head of Medusa, emblem of the black putrefaction which is indispensable to the alchemical process. Below she reappears in the guise of Iris (pl. 57); and on the right Venus stands on her scallop shell, her body all roses: the red flowering out of the white.

62 Above, Cerberus, the three-headed hound of Hell, devours the subject of the Work eight times over through the agency of the secret fire. Below, the subject, stripped of impurities (see pl. 27), is ready to be cooked in the Egg until perfection is reached.

Anon., 15th c., Biblioteca Apostolica Vaticana, Cod. Pal. lat. 1066, f. 224v., 227, 230v., 239.

Jmago Cupiditatis sic depingitur

Jmago auaricie sit depingitur

64

63 The White Rose is the whiteness that appears at the end of the Second Work.

Johannes Andreae, 15th century, British Museum, London, Sloane 2560, f. 14.

64 This illustration, which belongs to the period in which George Ripley lived, is a fitting counterpart to his 'Vision', and to Philalethes' commentary (see p. 23).

John Dastin, *De erroribus,* 15th century, British Museum, London, Egerton 845, f. 17v.

overleaf 65 'The bird of Hermes is my name, Eating my wings to make me tame.' This bird, preying on itself like Ouroboros (pl. 1) and the pelican (pl. 22), is an emblem of the cyclically sublimated mercury, which is said to drop a feather every time it rises.

Version of *Ripley Scrowle* by James Standysh, 16th c., B.M., London, Add. 32621 (detail).

HER·IS·THE·LAST·OF·THE·REDSTON

Documentary illustrations
and commentaries

1 The Royal or Sacerdotal Art

The illustrations to the *Philosophia reformata* of Mylius, published in 1622 in Frankfurt by Lucas Jennis, can be enjoyed independently of Mylius' prolix and recondite text; they constitute one of the finest collections of alchemical engravings in existence. Many of them have been used by other alchemists to illustrate their own texts.

A number of prime alchemical themes appear again and again in this sequence, notably those of the mystical wedding, death and resurrection, the conjunction of opposites, birth and exaltation. Many of the symbols, too, will be recognized: the lion and sun, Mercury with his caduceus, the king and queen, the dragon in the furnace, the arrow of the secret fire, the eagle, the androgyne, the triple serpent of dominion over the three realms. This whole sequence presents only a small part of the riches of alchemical imagery. In one sense, these engravings would take a lifetime to expound; and in another sense their coherence and imaginative power speak for themselves.

J.D. Mylius, *Philosophia reformata*, 1622, British Museum, London (Printed Books), 1033. i. 7, pp. 96, 107, 117, 126, 167, 190, 216, 224, 243, 262, 281, 300, 316, 354, 359, 361.

Putre facto.

4. Gradus.

11. Congelatio.

12. Cibatio.

13. Sublimatio.

14. Fermentatio.

15. Exaltatio.

16. Multiplicatio.

 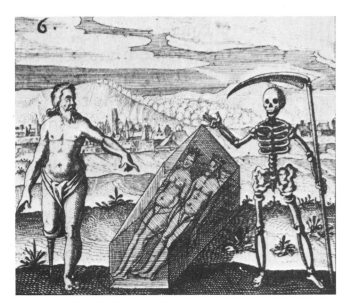

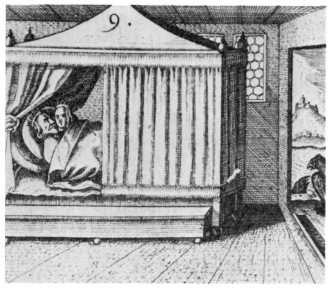

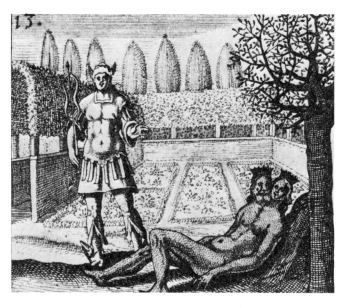

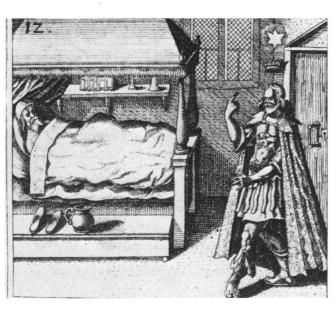

2 Eternal Transmigration

Such is the beauty of the *De summa* manuscript in the Arsenal, Paris, that it demands to be reproduced in its entirety. Two of the illustrations (xxxvii and xxxviii) are reproduced in colour as pls. 49 and 50.

The transmutation of the Elements is here fully illustrated; but, once more, not everything must be understood literally. Only two Elements are actually seen here, Earth containing Fire and Water containing Air, and it is these two that are converted. Water changes Earth into a liquid, which must in turn become Earth again. In the liquid state, the fixed is made volatile, and in being reduced to Earth the volatile is fixed. The eternal process of transmigration or sublimation is symbolized by the flight of the dove upwards and downwards. Conjunction and separation here are the so-called eagles, or repeated sublimations. These pairs of operations occur seven times in this manuscript, constituting the seven eagles which precede the exaltation of the Quintessence (pl. 50).

Sapientia veterum philosophorum sive doctrina eorundem de summa et universali medicina, 18th century, Bibliothèque de l'Arsenal, Paris, Ms. 974, fig. i–xxxvi, xxxix, xl.

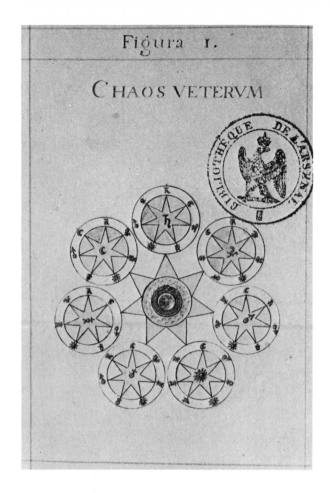

Figura III.

DISTILLATIO PHYSICA

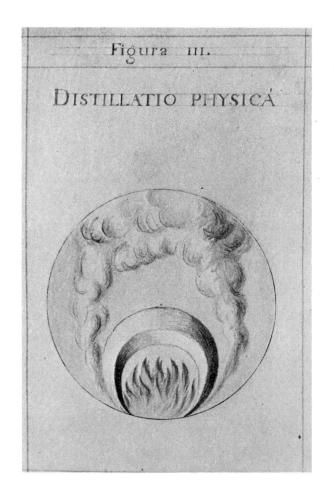

Figura IV.

PRÆPARATIO PHYSICA

Figura V.

DE DIVISIONE

Figura VI.

ACVATIO

Gabriel

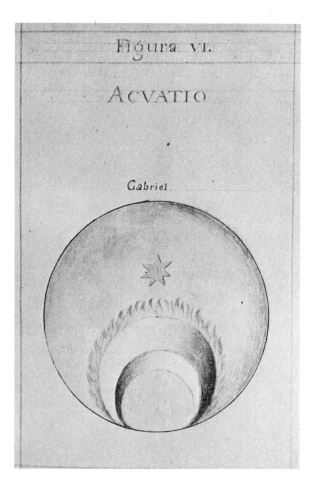

Figura VII.

LEO VIRIDIS

Figura VIII.

COITVS

Virtutes

Figura IX.

LAPIS TRI-VNVS

Figura X.

CALCINATIO

Figura XI.

SVBLIMATIO

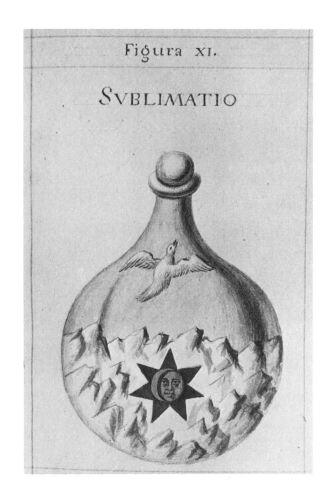

Figura XII.

SOLVTIO

Figura XIII.

GENERATIO

Figura XIV.

PVTREFACTIO

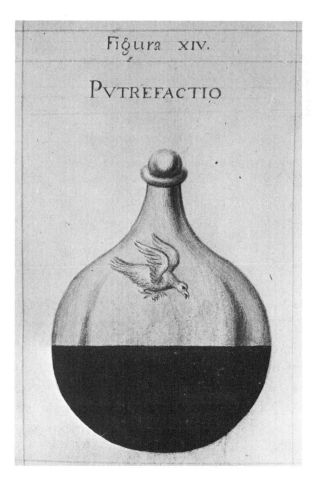

111

Figura xv.

CONCEPTIO

Figura xvi.

IMPRÆGNATIO

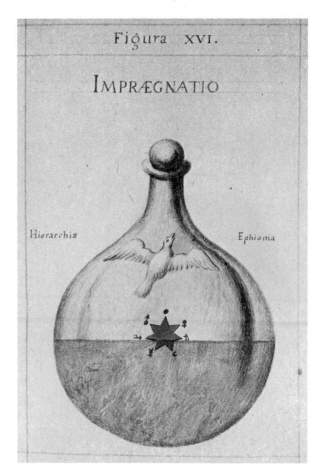

Hierarchiæ   Ephioma

Figura xvii.

FERMENTATIO

Figura xviii.

SEPARATIO

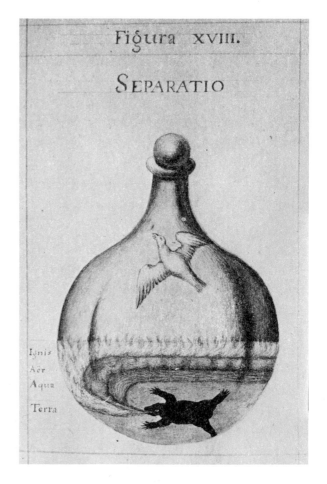

Ignis
Aër
Aqua
Terra

Figura XIX.

CONIVNCTIO

Ignis
Aer
Aqua
Terra

Figura XX.

SEPARATIO

Aqua
Aër
Ignis
Terra

Figura XXI.

CONIVNCTIO

Aqua in
Aër in A
Ignis
Terra

Aë
rem
quam

Figura XXII.

SEPARATIO

Ignis
Aqua
Aer
Terra

Figura XXIII.

CONIVNCTIO

Aer in
Ignis in
Aqua in
Terra

Ignem
Aquam
Aerem

Figura XXIV.

SEPARATIO

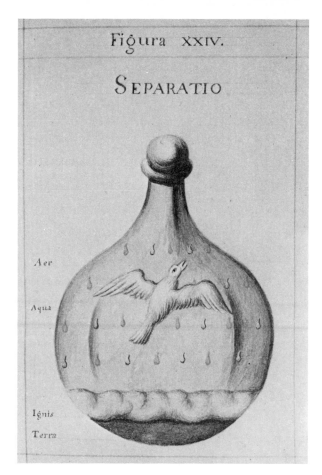

Aer
Aqua
Ignis
Terra

Figura XXV.

CONIVNCTIO. CŌMIXTIO

Ignis in
Aqua in
Aer in
Terra

Aerem
Ignem
Aquam

Figura XXVI.

SEPARATIO

Figura XXVII.

IGNIS INNATVRALIS

Figura XXVIII.

ORTVS

Figura XXIX.

FERMENTATIO

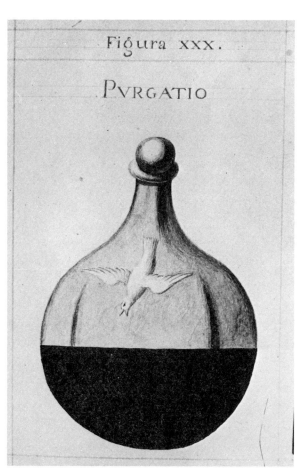

Figura XXX.

PVRGATIO

115

Figura XXXI.

SEPARATIO

Aqua in — Aerem
Ignis in — Aquam

Terra in — Ignem
Aqua Aer in — Terram

Figura XXXII.

CONIVNCTIO

Aër
Aqua
Ignis
Terra

Figura XXXIII.

SEPARATIO

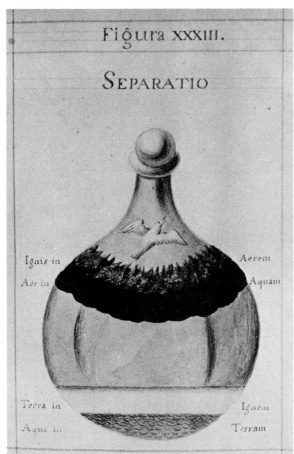

Ignis in — Aerem
Aer in — Aquam

Terra in — Ignem
Aqua in — Terram

Figura XXXIV.

CONIVNCTIO

Aër
Aqua
Ignis
Terra

Figura XXXV.

SEPARATIO

Terra in

Aer in

Aqua in

Ignis in

Aerem

Aquam

Ignem

Terram

Figura XXXVI.

CONIVNCTIO

Terra

Aer

Aqua

Ignis

Figura XXXIX.

FIXATIO

Figura XL.

PROIECTIO. CERATIO

3 The Progress of the Work

Plates 25–28 and 63 show early and late stages of the Work, from the raw chaos to the White and Red 'Roses'; the illustrations here, from the same manuscript, show some of the intermediate stages, together with quotations from the alchemical masters. The blackness will be recognized as that in which the subject is drowned (first illustration) and putrefies. The Raven's Head (*caput corvi*) signifies emergence from blackness (see pl. 17). Worms devouring each other signify, as Arnold of Villanova says, that the corruption of one is the generation of another; and within the Egg the earth is engulfed by the waters. The child which appears in the shadows of the Egg is Mercury; the Peacock's Tail appears above the white waters; from the ashes springs a seven-pointed flower.

Johannes Andreae, 15th century, British Museum, London, Sloane 2560, f. 8, 9, 10, 11, 12, 13.

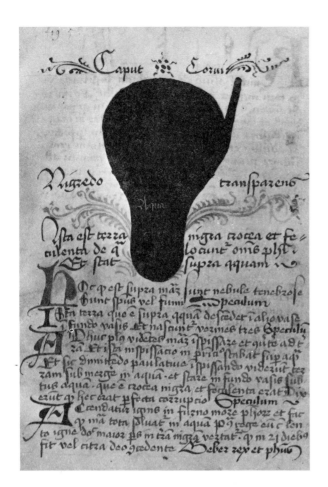

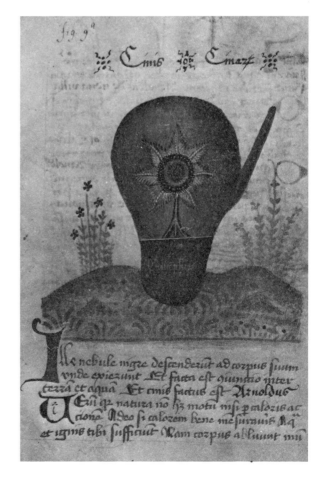

4 Cosmic diagrams

The *Sylva philosophorum* (see pls. 51–52) is described as follows by its author: 'An account of the universal tincture, or, of the Stone of the Wise, through the operation and power of which all imperfect metals can be brought to lasting perfection, being transmuted into gold and silver. That such Art is infallible and certain is demonstrated, in refutation of the detractors of this noble secret, and collected together for the benefit of all lovers of Nature, by Cornelius Petraeus of Hamburg, Student of the Hermetic Philosophy.' The diagrams represent, respectively: God (*Deus*), the Universe (*Macrocosmus*), the Four Elements (*Terra, Aer, Ignis, Aqua*), Man (*Homo*), Nature (*Natura*), the Soul (*Anima*), the Seed of the Work (*Semen*), and the Philosophers' Stone (*Lapis Philosophorum*).

The biblical text (this page, below) is taken from Deuteronomy XXXIII: 13–16. 'Blessed of the Lord be his land, for the precious things of heaven, for the dew, and for the deep that coucheth beneath. And for the precious fruits brought forth by the sun, and for the precious things brought forth by the moon. And for the chief things of the ancient mountains, and for the precious things of the lasting hills. And for the precious things of the earth and fulness thereof. . . .'

Cornelius Petraeus, *Sylva philosophorum,* 17th century, Bibliotheek der Rijksuniversiteit, Leiden, Cod. Voss. chem. q. 61, f. 1, 4–12.

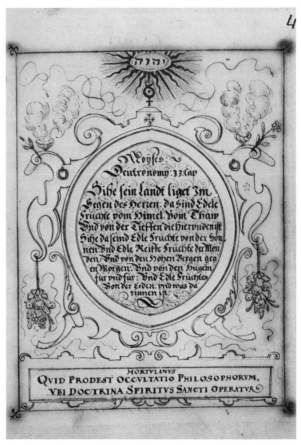

·I· FIGVRA·

DEVS EST VNVS, IN TRINITATE
ET TRINVS, IN VNITATE

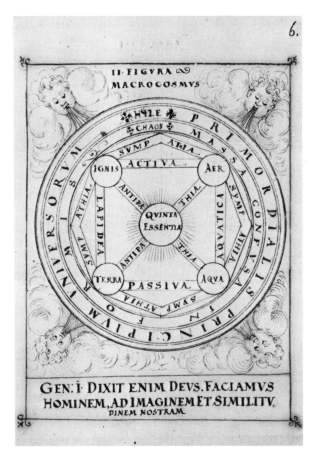

II·FIGVRA
MACROCOSMVS

GEN: I· DIXIT ENIM DEVS. FACIAMVS
HOMINEM, AD IMAGINEM ET SIMILITV·
DINEM NOSTRAM·

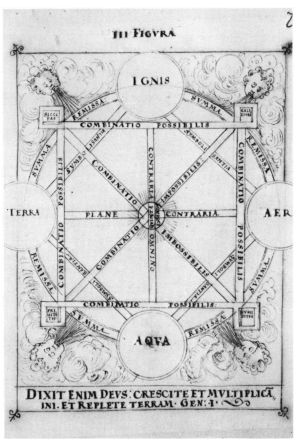

III FIGVRA

DIXIT ENIM DEVS: CRESCITE ET MVLTIPLICA,
INI. ET REPLETE TERRAM· GEN: I·

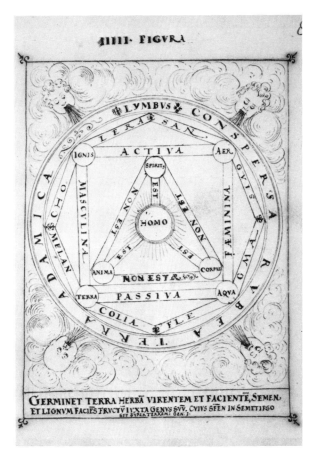

IIIII· FIGVRA

GERMINET TERRA HERBĀ VIRENTEM ET FACIENTĒ, SEMEN·
ET LIGNVM FACIĒS FRVCTV IVXTA GENVS SVV. CVIVS SĒEN IN SEMETIPSO
EST SVPER TERRAM: GEN: 2·

IIIIII FIGVRA

9

DEVS ET NATVRA NIHIL FACIVNT FRVSTRA

ANIMA LIS
NON EST EST NON EST
NATVRA
EST EST
VEGETA BILIS MINERA LIS
NON EST

NATVRA EST QVÆDAM RES, INSITA REBVS
EX SIMILIBVS SIMILIA PROCREANS

V.I. FIGVRA

10

OMNIA AB VNO OMNIA AD VNVM

RATIO NALIS
+MINERALIA EST HOMINES + VOLATILIA
ANIMA
+ANGELI EST
VEGETA TIVA SENSI TIVA
PLANTALIA + BRVTALIA

BERHARDVS: OMNE GENVS GENERAT SVVM SIMILE
IN NATVRA. NATVRALITER ET ARTIFICIALITER

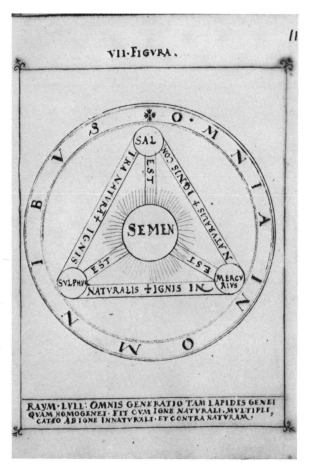

VII FIGVRA.

11

OMNIA IN OMNIBVS

SAL
EST
SEMEN
EST EST
SVLPHVR MERCV RIVS
NATVRALIS + IGNIS IN

RAYM. LVLL: OMNIS GENERATIO TAM LAPIDIS GENEI
QVAM HOMOGENEI. FIT CVM IGNE NATVRALI. MVLTIPLI,
CATÆO AB IGNE INNATVRALI. ET CONTRA NATVRAM.

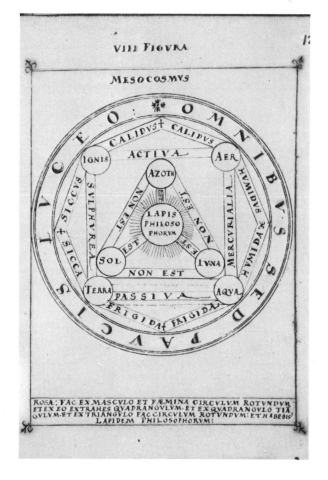

VIII FIGVRA

12

MESOCOSMVS

OMNIBVS SED PAVCIS

CALIDVS+ CALIDVS
IGNIS ACTIVA AER
AZOTH
NON EST NON EST
LAPIS PHILOSO PHORVM
EST EST
SOL LVNA
NON EST
TERRA PASSIVA AQVA
FRIGIDÆ FRIGIDA

ROSA: FAC EX MASCVLO ET FÆMINA CIRCVLVM ROTVNDVM
ET EX EO EXTRAHES QVADRANGVLVM. ET EX QVADRANGVLO TRI,
GVLVM. ET EX TRIANGVLO FAC CIRCVLVM ROTVNDVM: ET HABEBIS
LAPIDEM PHILOSOPHORVM:

122

5 The Operations

We have concentrated so far on the artistic and symbolic aspects of alchemical iconography. What follows is a collection of unusually precise technical diagrams of furnaces, aludels, crucibles and other pieces of equipment, which serves as a reminder that laboratory work cannot be dispensed with. There are two major ways or paths to choose from. The first, which is outlined on pp. 10–12 of this book, is called the Humid Way. It is longer than the other, but is preferred by many; its main feature is that the subject is sealed into a glass vessel. The Dry Way is considered faster, but as the manipulations are performed in an open mortar it is dangerous and requires a great deal of skill. Hints abound in the texts concerning a third or 'lightning' way, for which the operator must possess an incorruptible body capable of withstanding tremendous forces.

Anon., 15th century, British Museum, London, Harley 2407, f. 106v.–111.

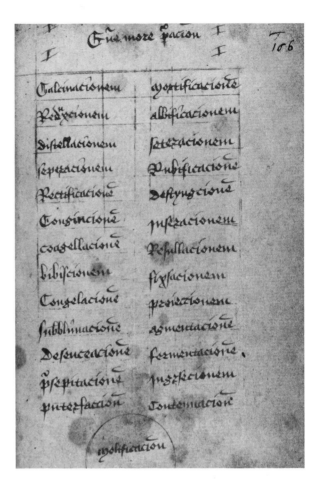

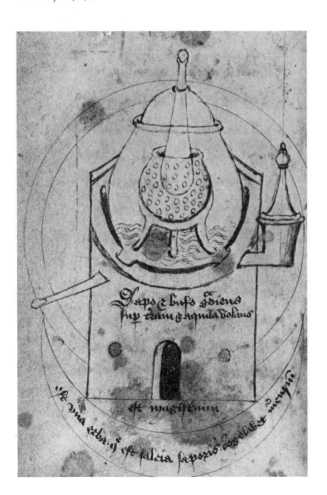

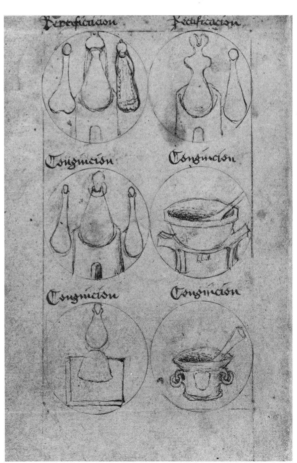

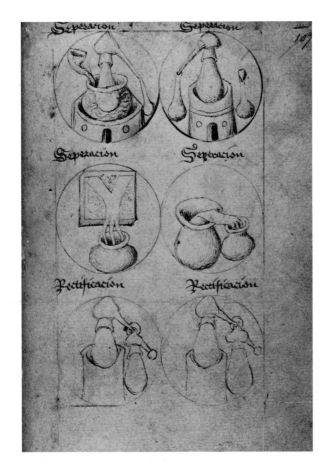

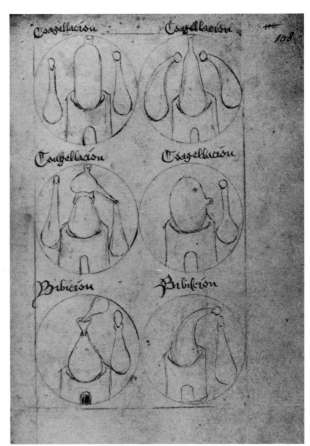

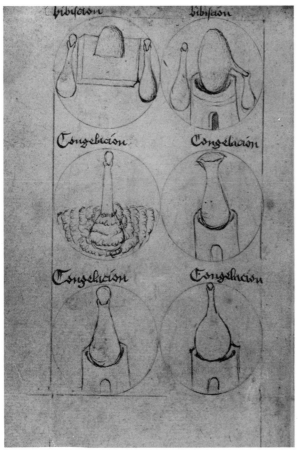

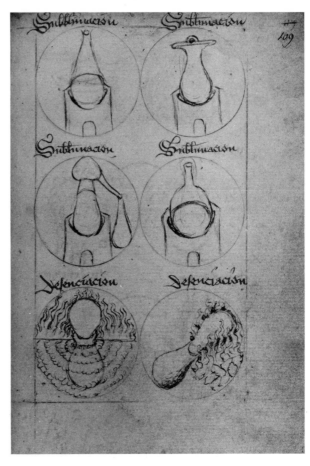

124

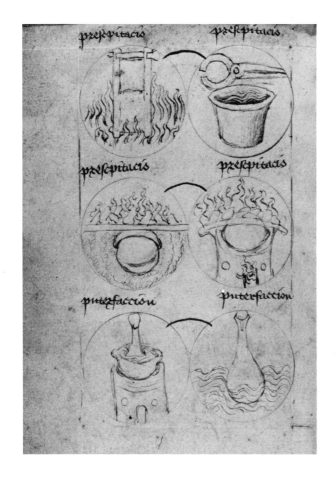

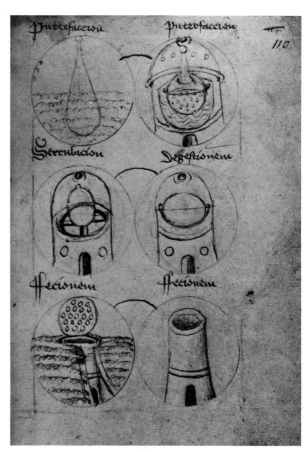

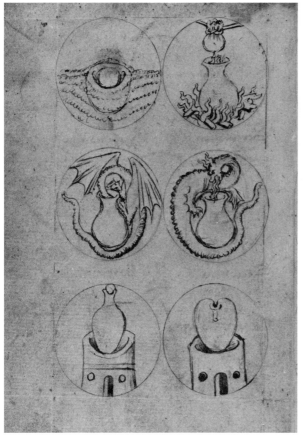

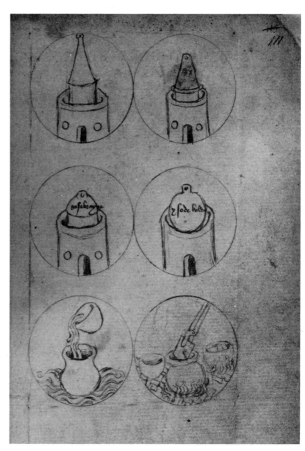

125

6 The Language of Symbols

This glossary is reproduced to give an idea of the variety of cryptic symbols used by the alchemists, who refer to them as the steganographic and spagyric signs. The symbols of the metals are followed by those of other chemical substances and of processes.

The introductory paragraph (below) is a reminder that the seven metals known to antiquity are likened to seven heavenly bodies. Gold (*aurum*) is the Sun (Sol); silver (*argentum*) is the Moon (Luna); quicksilver (*argentum vivum*) is Mercury; copper (*cuprum*) is Venus; tin (*stannum*) is Jupiter; lead (*plumbum*) is Saturn; iron (*ferrum*) is Mars. Other signs which frequently appear in alchemical art and literature include those of antimony (with its mysterious royal orb of dominion), fire (*ignis*), water (*aqua*), distillation, sublimation, solution, the harmoniac salt (*sal harmoniacum*, with its sign, the Star of Bethlehem; see pl. 44), and sulphur (see pl. 10). It must be remembered that all the names and symbols in alchemy have more than one meaning; very often, the substances referred to are 'not of the vulgar kind' (see also note to pl. 31).

Anon., 16th century, Bibliotheek der Rijksuniversiteit, Leiden, Cod. Voss. chem. q. 51, f. 1v.–3v.

Stagnum, Zinn Jupiter.

Plumbum, bley Saturnus.

Ferrum, Eisen Mars

Stahel

Antimonium,

[...]

[...]

[...]

Arsenicum

Auripigmentum

[...] Arsenicum

[...] Arsenicum

gelber Arsenicum

[...]

Crocum Martis Crocus

Crocum Veneris, [...]

Marcasita

Mercurium sublimati

Mercurium rubificati

Calcinati

Amalgama

Magnet

Element

[...]

[...]

[...] ignis

Aqua wasser

Monat

Tag

Nacht

Stratum superstratum

Distillation

Sublimation

Solution

[...]

[...]

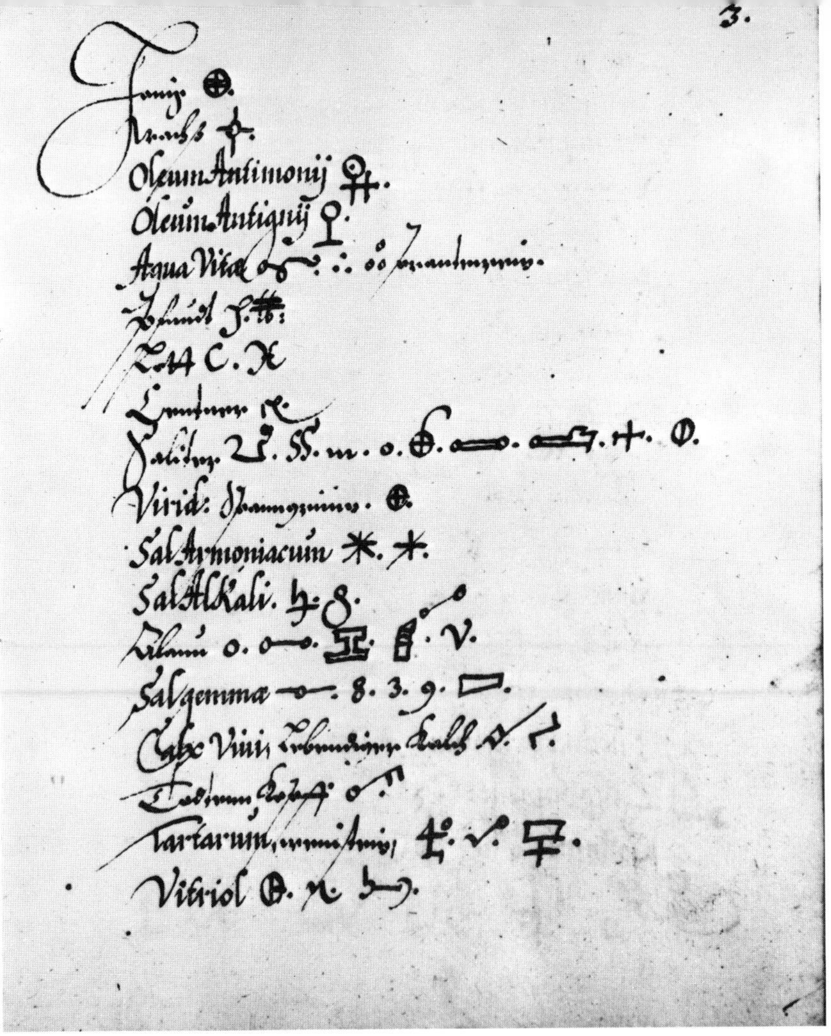

Ignis ⊕.

Aer ☿.

Oleum Antimonij ♃.

Oleum Antiquij ♀.

Aqua Vitæ ○ ∴ ÷ Brandewein.

� ꝶ℔꞉

Æs C. ✕

Saturnus ♃

Salnitru ♃ ℞ m . o . ⊖ ⊃ ⊂ . ⊶ ✠ . Ꝋ .

Viridi: Hispanicum . ⊕

Sal Armoniacum ✳ . ✱ .

Sal Alkali. ♄ . 𝟠 .

Alumen o . ⊶ . ⧈ ⬚ . υ .

Sal gemma ⊶ . 𝟠 . 𝟛 . ℈ . ▭ .

Calx Vivi Verbrandiner Kalck ∝ . ⅄ .

Sublimatum Sublimat ᴑ .

Tartarum Weinstein ⅄ . υ . ⯝ .

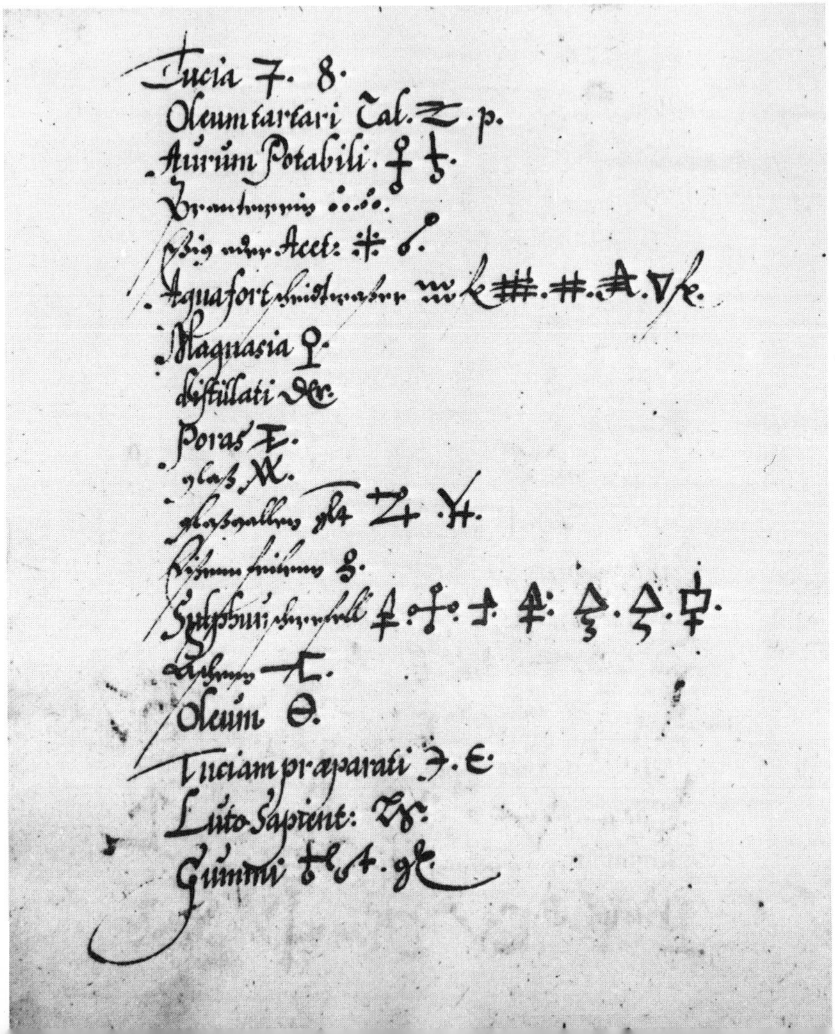

Vitriol ⊕ . ℞ . ⸰ .

Lucia 7 . 8 .

Oleum tartari Cal. ⚏ . p .

Aurum Potabili . ♀ ♄ .

Brandewein ∶ ∶ ∶

Scheidwaßer Acet: ✳ 𝟠 .

Aqua fort Scheidewaßer ℳ ꝶ # . ♯ . ♓ . ℣ ℞ .

Magnasia ♀ .

distillati ♒

Boras ⯮ .

Glaß ✕✕ .

Glaßgallen Glet ⚏ . ♃ .

Silber Siluer ♄ .

Sulphuris Schwefell ♃ . ◦♀ . ♇ . ⚴ . ♃ . ♀ . ⯝ .

Lithen ⯮ .

Oleum ⊖ .

Luciam præparati ꝫ . ϵ .

Luto Sapiente: ꝶ℣ .

Gummi ⅄℣ . gℛ .